God's Welcome

God's Welcome

HOSPITALITY FOR
A GOSPEL-HUNGRY WORLD

AMY G. ODEN

THE
PILGRIM
PRESS
Cleveland

The Pilgrim Press
700 Prospect Avenue
Cleveland, Ohio 44115-1100
thepilgrimpress.com

♻ Printed in the United States of America on acid-free paper that
contains post-consumer fiber.

16 15 14   9 8 7

Library of Congress Cataloging-in-Publication Data
Oden, Amy, 1958-
    God's welcome : hospitality for a gospel-hungry world /
Amy G. Oden.
      p.   cm.
    ISBN-13: 978-0-8298-1735-5 (alk. paper)
    1. Hospitality – Religious aspects – Christianity.   I. Title.
BV4647.H67O34 2008
241′.671 – dc22
                                                        2007040163

Scripture quotations are from:

The NEW REVISED STANDARD VERSION BIBLE, copyright © 1989 by the
Division of Christian Education of the National Council of the Churches of Christ
in the U.S.A., or

THE MESSAGE, copyright © 1993, 1994, 1995, 1996, 2000, 2001, 2002. Used by
permission of NavPress Publishing Group, or

The Holy Bible, NEW INTERNATIONAL VERSION. Copyright © 1973, 1978,
1984 International Bible Society. All rights reserved throughout the world. Used by
permission of International Bible Society.

Contents

Preface

What This Book Is About

This is a how-to book on hospitality, but not the kind that gives tips and tricks. This is the kind that gives roots. I believe the welcome we are all really hungry for is rooted in God's welcome. If our conversation on hospitality in the church stops with coffee pots and nametags, we are in danger of leaving folks hungry for the real food that brings them to our doors. When our congregations want to welcome the stranger, we start here, with a conversation about God's welcome. That's the gospel hospitality we offer to a gospel-hungry world. This is how-to book about staying rooted in God's welcome so that we can welcome others.

Chapter 1 introduces gospel hospitality as distinguished from hospitality in general. Gospel hospitality is God's welcome into abundant life, where all our welcome is rooted. Living in God's welcome we experience the marks of readiness, risk, repentance, and recognition. Chapter 2 looks at our experience of God's welcome in Scripture and in our lives. In chapter 3, we'll focus on how we can practice God's welcome in our everyday lives and in our congregational lives. Chapter 4 turns to a discussion of salvation as the theological language our tradition uses to talk about God's welcome. We'll look at Jesus as the primary pattern of that saving welcome into God's own life. Finally, some study group exercises give suggestions for ways to use this book in your church.

How I Came to Write This Book

I wrote this book because two trajectories in my life inter-sected. The first trajectory emerged in my own life of faith. I was increasingly alarmed that the face of Christianity in the United States was becoming unwelcoming. Along with so many others, I wondered why Christian voices in the media, in politics, and in our local communities were increasingly neg-ative, even hostile. This face of Christianity failed to present the good news of hope and abundant life. Christianity is, at its very heart, a welcoming faith, proclaiming a welcoming God in Jesus Christ. To the degree that Christians have strayed from this center, I want to reclaim our roots in God's welcome.

The second trajectory emerged in my life as a historian of the church. I've spent the last few years researching the prac-tices of hospitality in the early Christian world (the fruits of which you can read in my book *And You Welcomed Me*)[1] in order to understand how early Christians struggled with wel-coming the stranger. Why did they bother? What did they actually do? One of the big discoveries in that research was how radically early Christians practiced hospitality, not be-cause they were trying to be good, but because they were profoundly moved by God's welcome in their own lives and wanted to share it in concrete ways — tending to the conta-gious sick that no one would help, receiving foreign refugees seeking aid, welcoming the poor and outcasts in their com-munities. They offered hospitality because they believed God really had new and abundant life to offer everyone. My time with these ancient faithful ones over the last few years has brought home to me the stark contrast between their under-standing of hospitality and our own brand today, which can sometimes border on Wal-Mart greeter-ism.

---

1. Amy Oden, *And You Welcomed Me: Sourcebook on Hospitality in Early Christianity* (Nashville: Abingdon Press, 2001).

These two trajectories, the distressing portrayal of Christianity as unwelcoming in the current culture, and the rich lessons we have from ancient Christians about hospitality, came together in my life and in this book. There's no doubt in my mind that contemporary Christians want to be welcoming. Like our ancient Christian family, we can return to our most basic experience of God's welcome in order to find our way as a community of hospitality.

The world is hungry for God's welcome and we dare not withhold the food. If thoughtful Christians allow the gospel of fear and hostility to masquerade as Christianity, we let people starve. This book is an invitation to live in God's welcome and to proclaim it to the world.

Who I Need to Thank

God's welcome in my life has been deep and wide, and has been made known through the hands and hearts of so many who bless my life. Thanks to the faculty, staff, and students of Wesley Theological Seminary in Washington, DC, a community of deep hospitality that gives me great hope for the future of the church. Thanks to the congregation of Wesley Freedom United Methodist Church in Sykesville, Maryland, for providing a welcoming community. Thanks to the Academy for Spiritual Formation for the opportunity to say out loud and subsequently shape my thoughts for this book, all in wonderful Red Rock Canyon, Oklahoma. For invaluable help with the writing and organization of the book, I want to thank Timothy Staveteig, Ulrike Guthrie, Jane Donovan, Jean Link, Susan Ross, Jeni Markham Clewell, Beth Ream, Perry Williams, Andy Oden, and Jane Oden. Finally, I am blessed with a family who lives the welcoming life. I give thanks to God for all the Oden clan, and also especially my husband, Perry Williams, and son, Walker Lindley.

Chapter 1

Gospel Hospitality

The word "hospitality" buzzes through our congregations. What does it mean? Being friendly to visitors? Having a coffee time after church? Posting signs out front that promise our openness? Hospitality is all these things — and much more.

Gospel Hospitality Defined

Gospel hospitality is God's welcome, a welcome that is deep and wide. Gospel hospitality is God's welcome into a new way of seeing and living. Ultimately, gospel hospitality is God's welcome into abundant life, into God's own life. Scripture is packed with stories of hospitality, stories of God's own welcome sometimes through a host, often through a guest or stranger, a welcome that is often full of surprises, for both host and guest. Gospel hospitality almost always entails some kind of risk and leaves all parties changed. As we participate in gospel hospitality, God's welcome becomes a way of life that we share with the world.

This description may produce nods of agreement. Nothing new here, it would seem. Gospel hospitality has always been at the heart of the Christian life. God's welcome to every creature is a biblical proclamation and is the good news that we preach. But how do we move from knowledge of God's welcome to action? In this book, gospel hospitality will be the key to help us uncover and recover the present reality we all know and live, God's welcome deep in the heart of faith.

What's for Dinner?

We've gotten much better at inviting people over for dinner. In the last decade churches have put a lot of effort into greeting visitors, improving signs, and offering visitors the closest parking spots, providing large print bulletins and informational brochures, creating websites and church banners that are inviting. These frontline efforts help us cultivate friendliness and warmth, drawing our attention to strangers. This is hard work, and we're doing a better job than we ever have.

Once our guests arrive, what's for dinner? Greeting is only the first step of hospitality. Gospel hospitality calls us to the next step beyond greeting: feeding. If we're not careful, we'll get really good at inviting people over, but have nothing to feed them when they arrive. You can imagine the skepticism with which you would view a host who invited you over, had decorated for a party, made sure the steps and doorway were well lit, but hadn't actually prepared anything to eat. Such a welcome rings hollow and thin.

As Christian people, we have food to share with a world that is hungry, even famished. Spiritual wanderers — those spiritually starved and denied — show up at our doors, not because they like our buildings or even because they like us, but because they are hungry. Hungry for forgiveness, for rest and peace. Hungry for mercy and grace. Hungry to explore and grow. Hungry for the good news of new life, of abundant life. Hungry for God to do a new thing.

Gospel hospitality offers welcome food. We feed on the grace of God every moment of every day and welcome others to the table. Gospel hospitality calls us beyond friendliness to share the solid food that blesses our lives. Gospel hospitality welcomes strangers not just into the church, but into God's life. Always, always, it is *God's* welcome that we offer.

Both Sides of Gospel Hospitality

Josh had been shuffled from his mom's home to relatives' homes, and through foster homes, for as long as he could remember. Now at sixteen he was living with the father of one of his half-brothers. Josh was one of eight children of a drug-addicted mother, with little stability in his life. This year was his first full school year in one place. Josh had always been labeled learning disabled, had never really been able to fit into a classroom, and was often a behavioral problem for teachers. Equally hard for Josh had been finding friends. He was seen as marginal and dangerous by most of his peers, so the only kids open to him were other kids identified as marginal and dangerous, too. His social experiences had been troubled and limited.

When a youth from our church invited Josh to our youth group, Josh was suspicious: "What do they want? They're all a bunch of religious snobs who think they're better than everyone else. They don't want me there." On his first visit to youth group, he played Frisbee and it was okay. Youth ran around, yelling and playing, and they closed with prayer where several kids lifted concerns about their own lives and their friends' lives. No one snubbed him, though some of the youth were surprised to see him there. The next Sunday, Adam offered to pick him up for church, so Adam and Josh came together to the contemporary worship, an informal and upbeat service with lots of youth participation. Josh was shocked at the friendliness, the ease of interaction, kids wearing everything from tattered jeans to dresses, even some with piercings. He didn't stand out, and people seemed to accept him as he was. The following weeks, Josh came back to church and to youth group and experienced acceptance like he had never known. He was surprised by the honesty of youth in sharing their struggles and questions. Josh joined in Bible study and explored prayer as a conversation with God. Josh was fed.

Some months later, when he asked to be baptized and join the church, Josh admitted that his initial reaction to this welcome was disbelief. Was it for real or just an act? As he came to know the welcome was real, in the experience of deep hospitality Josh started to see himself as someone welcomed not only by this church, but by God. Josh started to see himself as a child of God, loved and received into God's life, even someone with gifts to bring and share. This is the transformative power of hospitality.

Gospel hospitality isn't just about the newcomer. It's also about those doing the welcoming, those already in the church, and this story is no exception. The same gospel hospitality that had touched Josh transformed the youth group, too. Several youth reported how their experiences with Josh had changed them. Caitlynn, a high school sophomore, said that hearing Josh's family circumstance and struggles gave her new eyes to see her own family and their struggles. Daniel said that Josh's enthusiasm for Bible study gave him fresh eyes to read the Scripture passages he'd heard all his life. For Sarah, it was Josh's heartfelt appreciation for what a youth group, or any Christian community bound by love, could be. This experience of gospel hospitality spilled over to the halls of the high school, where the strict pecking order of insiders and outsiders governs so much of life. Caitlynn, Daniel, and Sarah began to see how the insider/outsider categories functioned in their own lives, and began to cross boundaries — in the lunchroom, in study groups, even in choosing with whom to sit at school assemblies. Welcoming Josh meant welcoming a new set of eyes into their lives, so that God's welcome into a deeper, more abundant life was theirs, too. This is the transformative power of hospitality.

We might say it this way: at its deepest, hospitality points to God. You know this in your own experience. The deepest welcomes, often unexpected, profoundly shape our views of ourselves, of others, and of God. Maybe you experienced deep hospitality as a young parent with unruly children in church when a smiling usher offered crayons and coloring pages. You may have experienced it as a recently divorced person, unsure of whether other Christians would see you as a failure, yet finding a place of welcome and healing. Or you may have known the transformative power of hospitality as one who had been estranged from God and from the church for many years and who was very wary about stepping back in. Yet in your first tentative steps, you were met more than half way by a church family that affirmed your questions and explorations as all being part of God's life.

Unfortunately, there are many — too many — in our pews who have never known deep welcome, at least not in church. For many of us, our deepest welcomes didn't happen in church at all. The forgiveness extended by an estranged family member, the quiet presence of a friend during chemotherapy, the reassuring recognition by those who love us for who we really are when we have lost our way: these are the experiences that make plain to us God's welcome, experiences that open doors and change lives, experiences that reorient our hearts. The point of gospel hospitality is to invite others to experience the living, welcoming God and to experience the living, welcoming God in others.

Under the Oaks of Mamre (Genesis 18:1-15)

The Bible tells a story of gospel hospitality in Genesis. Abraham had been standing outside his tent watching the road most of the morning, when he spied a shape in the distance.

Travelers happened along this road only every ten days or so. It wasn't so much that he knew anyone was coming today as that he wanted to be ready in case someone was. They had settled their tent under the sheltering oaks at Mamre years ago. It was to this place God had called them when Abraham and Sarah left behind the life they had known and set out on a life journey to an alien place. Here Melchizedek, the priest of the Most High God, had pronounced blessing on them. Here God had promised as many descendants as the countless stars. How many nights he and Sarah had looked up, silently holding hands, aching for this promise to be fulfilled! But decades have gone by, Abraham now in his nineties, Sarah in her eighties, and they have stopped waiting for a child.

As three figures come into view, Abraham runs out to them, bowing low and begging them to do him the favor of stopping for a rest at his home. He directs them to the shade under the tree, already shouting out instructions for food and drink. He washes their feet and serves the three strangers himself, an unusual role for the man of the house. In fact, he stands by waiting upon them while they eat.

As the guests finish eating and wipe their mouths, they turn to ask Abraham about his wife, Sarah. Sarah, who is in the tent where she has been working all along, perks up her ears at the shocking idea that strange men should ask after her. One of the strangers, the ancient one with burning eyes, says the most amazing thing: when he returns next year, Sarah will have a son. The notion that this feeble one would be coming back by their tent next year was outlandish enough. The notion that Sarah would bear a child is downright outrageous, even cruel. But this news is so implausible that Sarah can only laugh. These are strange strangers indeed. Is this some sort of trick? Will God's promise really come to pass?

As it turns out, these strangers — welcomed and refreshed — bring a surprising and unbelievable gift. They enter the picture as guests, the ones receiving welcome, but as the story unfolds, they become hosts, the ones offering welcome to Abraham and Sarah into a whole new life as parents. What's for dinner is not only food but hope.

Marks of Gospel Hospitality

Early Christians point to the story of Abraham and Sarah under the oaks of Mamre as the paradigmatic story of hospitality, its quirks and its blessings. Christians have looked to this story for the particular characteristics of the radical hospitality God offers — readiness, risk, repentance, and recognition. Abraham, Sarah, and the strange travelers lay bare for us these spiritual marks of gospel hospitality.

My husband is an avid hiker and marches headlong down a path, seemingly never flustered or lost. In contrast, I have to stop and get my bearings repeatedly. How can I know I'm still on the right path? How can I know which way to go? He explained to me that the hiking trails are marked by blazes, patches of bright paint on tree trunks that are color-coded for the various paths. The yellow blazes, or marks, let me know I am indeed on the yellow path. The blue blazes mark the blue path. Reassuring signs to mark the way. So it is with the spiritual marks of hospitality. When we see these marks, we know we are on the path of gospel hospitality. These marks are signposts along the way. They flag the reorientations of heart that follow wherever gospel hospitality leads.

Readiness: Expecting Strangers

In the story from Genesis 18, Abraham is standing at the door of his tent, ready. He is watching, expectant. He doesn't know who is coming or when, but he doesn't want to miss it when they arrive. Notice, Abraham does not pace up and down the road. He doesn't start out on a journey to go find strangers he can bring home. He's not holed up within the safe walls of his tent. He's ready and steps outside the door of the tent to watch.

Early Christians read this story of the strangers at Mamre to mean that whether we are guests or hosts we need to be ready — ready to welcome, ready to enter another's world, ready to be vulnerable. This readiness is expectant. It may be akin to moral nerve. It exudes trust: trust that opportunities to welcome are just around the corner, trust that offering welcome will draw us closer to God, trust that participation in hospitality is participation in the life of God.

Abraham's readiness doesn't just appear one morning. Readiness comes from practice and experience walking with God. Before the story of the strangers at Mamre, the previous chapters of Genesis chronicle Abraham's radical openness to the call of God on his life, leaving all he had known and going to an alien land sight unseen. Readiness has taken root in his life. The readiness that marks gospel hospitality comes from a lifetime of listening to God and opening our hearts. Readiness is a way of life in God's life, so that when the strangers appear, readiness has already taken root.

For us, in order to be ready to offer gospel hospitality, we may have some groundwork to lay first. Like Abraham, we will have to listen to God and open our hearts. The more we pay attention to our own experiences of God's welcome in our lives, the more ready we are to participate in gospel hospitality. This attentiveness to God's welcome in our congregations gives readiness deep roots so that when the stranger arrives, we are open.

Without such readiness, our hospitality is a house built on sand, swamped by the first wave of disappointment or rejection. Hospitality not marked by readiness can do damage because it is a welcome that cannot make good on its claims.

Too many people have been hurt when a church offered a welcome that turned out to be only a couple of visits deep. The gospel is hurt by unready hospitality. It's important to be clear about what it is we are ready for. I'd suggest that ready hearts trust not so much that we will succeed in some particular outcome, but that God will do a new thing. Such readiness takes courage, gratitude, and radical openness.

What does readiness to welcome others look like in our congregational lives? It shows up in all sorts of ways. Readiness is expressed in the openness of the worship team to youth who want to lead, or in the young father who invites to church a single dad and his son from the soccer team he coaches. While it will vary with each context, as an orientation of the heart, readiness is attentive and observant, so that strangers are not invisible or ignored. Readiness is intentional and humble. Readiness is expressed in the greeter at the door who genuinely welcomes from the heart. Abraham did not drag the strangers from the road. The greeter doesn't go into the parking lot to pull people from their cars. Readiness does not burden the stranger with our need for approval or acceptance. Readiness expects God's welcome to transform both host and guest. Ready hearts look for opportunities to extend God's welcome, expecting God to be at work.

For further exploration of readiness, see Meditations 2, 5, 7, and 8 in chapter 3.

Risk: Disruptive and Dangerous

Because hospitality has become sentimentalized in recent centuries, we tend to associate it with being comfortable, with warm and fuzzy feelings. We can easily miss the reality, understood so well by biblical accounts and early Christians, that hospitality is disruptive and dangerous.

The first risk Abraham takes may be the hardest one for us: he risks rejection. What if the strangers say no? We do not know whether the strangers would have stopped under the oaks of Mamre if Abraham had not invited them. We only know that Abraham invites them, actually begs them, to stop and receive his hospitality. For Abraham and Sarah and their extended family, the next risk is the very concrete risk of physical danger: three grown men could easily overpower an aged Abraham and Sarah. Welcome also carries the risks of theft or even disease. They cannot know the outcomes of their actions in welcoming the travelers. Given the dangers, why take the risks of hospitality at all? We are not told the motivations of the various characters, but we are told in the opening verse that "the Lord appears" under the oaks of Mamre (Gen. 18:1). God's presence gives courage for the risk hospitality entails.

Welcoming the stranger puts oneself and one's community at risk. At best, the stranger is disruptive, bringing strange ideas and new, even wrong, ways of doing things. At worst, the stranger is dangerous, bringing disease, dishonor, or violence. Welcoming the stranger is risky: everyone will be changed, host and guest alike, as Abraham and Sarah attest. Nothing will be the same anymore, and we cannot know ahead of time what the changes will be.

We can no longer maintain a status quo, keep things as they are, because the stranger brings a new frame of reference. All of this spells unexpected outcomes, for individuals and for communities. Hospitality asks us for a deep trust that God is at work, both in the host and in the stranger. Ultimately, it is God doing the welcoming. Risk can be scary, but when it accompanies welcoming, it's likely we're on the path of gospel hospitality. If we risk nothing, it is unlikely we are participating in God's welcome.

In our own time, the risks of hospitality are real and can quickly swamp the boat of enthusiasm in our churches. We may warm to the idea of welcoming children into an after-school program at our church until we realize the liability insurance the church will have to purchase, the extended custodial services due to much harder wear and tear on the building, and the general chaos that results from children in the building all week. All of these factors put the congregation at risk financially and perhaps missionally.

Or take another example: We begin a campaign to invite those from the neighborhood surrounding our church to join us on Sunday morning. We canvass the neighborhood with flyers and have a big kickoff festival on the church grounds. After some initial interest from three or four families in the neighborhood, we now have almost twenty neighborhood children ages four to twelve attending on Sunday morning — but without their parents, a situation we hadn't counted on. Our hearts are in the right place, but the risks of hospitality are sobering.

For many congregations, the risk of hospitality is expressed in the question, What if it doesn't work? Risk of failure can paralyze us. Of course, this requires us to think through what success and failure mean when we offer God's welcome. Is it possible to fail? Abraham's only goal seems to be for the strangers to allow him to offer hospitality. Neither Abraham nor Sarah sees success as getting the strangers to join their family or follow their God or pass on the word about what great hospitality they received. In fact, Abraham's invitation includes the recognition that the strangers will have refreshment and then "be on your way." We usually get stuck in measuring our hospitality by others' response to it, or by our own desired outcome. Genesis 18 teaches us that hospitality, risks and all, is God's doing. Our hearts, then, take risks in order to be faithful, to trust in God's leading, regardless of outcome. Risk is a spiritual mark of hospitality.

A caution: risk as a mark of gospel hospitality is not to be confused with reckless abandon. Risk is clear-eyed, not sentimental or impulsive. The risks of hospitality bring gifts as well as demands. The risks of hospitality humble us, remind us we rely on God's welcome for courage, and force us to stay openhanded, ready to receive whatever outcome results.

For further exploration of risk see Meditations 3, 4, 5, 9, 10, and 13 in chapter 3.

Repentance: Not Regret but Turning

Gospel hospitality is marked by new life, by change and transformation, not by business as usual. Welcoming the stranger inevitably brings challenges to our life together. Scripture describes this new life with the word "repentance," but not to mean "feel bad" or "feel sorry," describing an emotional state of regret as we typically use it today.

The biblical notion of repentance is much more active. It means changing one's mind, or turning, literally changing direction from one path to another. Abraham and Sarah experience a turning. They have been on the road of despair for decades, waiting for a promised child who never came. In fact, giving up on this hoped-for child, Sarah authorizes her servant, Hagar, to bear a son on her behalf (Gen. 16:1ff.). In Genesis 18, the strangers bring news that requires Sarah and Abraham to turn onto a new path, a hope path. Of course, they are at first skeptical about whether such a path exists; indeed, Sarah finds it laughable. Still, they both turn from resignation to expectation, a repentance (turning) that will bear great fruit. The hosts in this story encounter strangers, and the hosts themselves are turned, changed.

So forget about surface welcomes in which two persons do not take each other seriously, such as the pleasantry, "Hi, how are you?" Such surface welcomes change no one; indeed, they often do not even expect the other's reply. Think instead about the sort of welcome that sees the world in a new way — that sees through the eyes of the other. Consider your own experiences of welcoming others. You know that you have been changed by your encounters, and that's what repentance is all about. We approach the edge of the unfamiliar and cross it, if only by a step. When we are received into God's life and, in turn, receive others, we encounter something new, whether we are the host or the guest. We know we are on the path of gospel hospitality when we experience this turning.

Take, for example, a college professor named Don, who participated in his college's international student program. He signed up to be an "American friend" to Ahmed, a new student from Pakistan, and included Ahmed in several family activities to help him get acquainted with American culture. By far the most difficult to explain was Halloween as Ahmed watched variously dressed children come to Don's door and "trick or treat!" Throughout the year, Don believed he was practicing Christian hospitality; he was the host welcoming the stranger.

But that wasn't the end of the story. The following year after 9/11, Ahmed had to get his name on a list of "cleared" foreign students in order to continue his studies. As a young Pakistani male, Ahmed seemed to be under suspicion everywhere he went. He wouldn't be able to visit his family or travel until his name was on the cleared list. His attempts to get on the list went on for months, and eventually Ahmed turned to Don for help. Don accompanied Ahmed to various government offices to try to get answers, only to be turned away time and again. Don's experience with Ahmed gave Don a new perspective on being a foreigner in America, especially a

Muslim. Don said he would never watch the news the same way again. He would never hear what others said about Muslims the same way. He had glimpsed the world through the eyes of Ahmed, and it decentered his worldview, causing a turn. Gospel hospitality decenters us, turns our lives around. If our lives remain unchanged/unturned, we're probably not practicing gospel hospitality.

A welcome that takes the other seriously requires me to shift from the way I see things to the way the other person sees things. When I see the world through the other's eyes, I cannot simply return to my old way of seeing. This shift invariably leads to repentance, because I see the degree to which my own view had become the only view. The sense one has of being comfortable with the way things are is shaken up by this new frame of reference. One can no longer be at home in quite the same way. These new "eyes to see" give a new frame of reference, bigger than we had before.

When we welcome others, something happens to us. We are changed by the welcome we offer, as God fills and reorients our hearts. This decentering and reframing is the very movement the New Testament calls *metanoia,* or turning, usually translated "repentance." This turning and repentance occurs not only in the interior landscape of the individual, but also in the exterior landscape of the community. As communities become more hospitable they experience a turning, too. While it may not always be easy, the mark of repentance assures us we are on the path of gospel hospitality.

For further exploration of repentance, see Meditations 3, 4, 6, 7, and 12 in chapter 3.

Recognition: Eyes to See Christ

When Abraham sees the three men, he addresses them with deference, claims to be their servant, and begs them to stop at his tent for refreshment. He gives them the very best he has, "choice flour" and "calf, tender and good" (v. 7). Who does Abraham think these men are? Why the royal treatment? The story doesn't say exactly, only that he calls them "Lord." Of course, we, as readers, are told from the beginning in verse 1 that "The LORD appeared to Abraham under the oaks of Mamre," so we are expecting something special. How did Abraham know? How did he recognize them as perhaps more than they appeared to be? Later, explaining this episode, Hebrews says, "Do not neglect to show hospitality to strangers, for by doing that some have entertained angels without knowing it" (Heb. 13:2).

Abraham recognized these strangers as more than simply strangers. He could have seen the three men and quickly concluded: these are merchants on their way to market, drifters looking for a hand-out, or con men looking for an easy mark. Abraham concludes none of these things, and instead treats the strangers as honored guests.

Recognition is more than just seeing. Recognition is seeing deeply, seeing beyond what appears to be. It's a recalling, a remembering, a seeing again. Abraham is able to see past appearances to the holy presence within them, to know them. When God values us truly or recognizes us as God's children, rather than as strangers, God sees beyond our appearances. God recognizes us for who we really are. When we recognize strangers as Jesus, we too see beyond appearances. Gospel hospitality is marked by such recognition.

Jesus is often described as seeing beyond appearances. When Jesus talks to the woman at the well (John 4) he recognizes her as more than she appears. When Jesus later asks the disciples, "Who do you say that I am?" he is calling them to see beyond appearances, to recognition (Matt. 16:15, Mark 8:29, Luke 9:20). We've all had the experience of another person recognizing in us something greater than we ourselves could see: The teacher who could see our potential when we struggled in school. The supervisor who knew we could handle more responsibility. The mentor who took our dreams seriously, envisioning the people we could become.

The longing for recognition, to be seen for our deepest, truest selves, is always just below the surface of appearances. When a harried young mother is at odds with her child in the grocery checkout line, but the cashier talks to her as the loving, committed mother she is, the mother feels valued. When an unemployed man shows up for an interview and the interviewer sees him as the capable, employable man he is, the man is appreciated. We all know the pain of not being seen for who we truly are, of being labeled and dismissed. That's why it is so powerful to see ourselves or others through God's eyes. That is the truest recognition and the deepest welcome of all. When we see people in categories — young black man, tattooed teenager, soccer mom, older white guy — we too easily miss the truth that each brings Christ if we but have eyes to see.

This kind of recognition helps us truly feel welcome. Some Christians have begun to talk of "otherliness" as a Christian discipline, a way of seeing and serving the other. No doubt the kind of deep seeing that hospitality invokes takes time and patience. To recognize the presence of Christ in another may not happen quickly. It often requires getting to know them, taking time to look beyond their clothes, employment, language, manners, or needs. We may need to listen to the testimony of another, some of their life story, to fully appreciate Christ's presence within them. We may have to work together or pray together before we begin to recognize another. We may also have to modify our idea of what Jesus looks like in order to recognize Christ in another.

Recognizing Christ in another is, in itself, a proclamation of the good news of God's welcome. Such recognition proclaims that God is already present and that each person is a precious gift who cannot be reduced to labels or social categories. Recognition sees beyond what appears to be to what truly is. Recognition speaks to our deepest longings to be seen and known, and is at the heart of hospitality. Abraham had eyes to see deeply and indeed the strangers were considerably more than they appeared to be, bringing God's promise to fulfillment. The mark of recognition signals that we are on the path of hospitality.

For further exploration of recognition, see Meditations 3, 4, 5, 8, 11, and 14 in chapter 3.

The Stakes

Why pay attention to gospel hospitality? So much is at stake! So many people hunger for mercy, for abundant life, but are left empty-handed. So many people are excluded, noses pressed against the windows of God's life, not knowing how to get in. Most of them believe they aren't welcome inside — because they aren't good enough, or don't read the Bible enough, or aren't Christian enough. When we fail to make plain God's welcome to all people, or are indifferent to making it plain, we leave them on the outside looking in. The pain and suffering of the world cry out for each of us and all of us to say, "God's welcome is at hand!" "You are God's precious, beloved child. Welcome." God's heart melts for those hungering after mercy and God's heart breaks when we withhold it.

Meet Stan, who has been attending a church for several weeks because co-workers have told him about the church. He has found it to be a friendly enough place and has made an appointment to talk with the pastor. As he enters, he is nervous. After pleasantries, the pastor invites Stan to be seated. They discuss Stan's work. Then Stan halts and his brow furrows. "But, you know, I still don't feel at home around church,

any church, really." As the pastor listens, Stan recounts all
he'd been taught about the Christian life — how God loved
him and wanted him to follow God's ways and God's will.
In fact, Stan shares that he had grown up the son of de-
vout Christian parents, so that his parents' expectations were
often synonymous with God's. As a child, he was always anx-
ious about making God mad at him, or his parents mad at
him. He felt as if he could never do enough, never be good
enough. He knew there were always minor failures or over-
sights. How could he be a truly good Christian? By his teen
years, he began to see that most of the so-called "Christian"
adults around him had their own flaws, and he concluded that
Christian faith was just a sham, a bunch of talk used to try
to make people follow the rules. If God couldn't be satisfied
with Stan's efforts, then forget it. Stan said that by college he
had wiped his hands clean of this temperamental God.

Now Stan's face just looks sad. "I know there's more to life,
and I want it. I feel this pull . . . but to what? I don't know.
And I don't trust this whole Christian thing. I'm probably not
supposed to say that to a pastor, but there it is." The more
Stan talks, the more his pain and anger come out about the
manipulations of a God who puts up hoops for people to jump
through and about his own sense of failure and feeling lost.

How often have we in our churches failed to fully make
plain God's welcome, unconditional, into new life? Stan was
on the outside looking in. For every Stan who can speak
about his alienation from God, there are hundreds of others
who cannot. For every Stan who knows he longs for more,
there are hundreds for whom such longing rests just below
consciousness.

At stake in gospel hospitality is the prevalent view, con-
firmed too often, that Christianity is an unwelcoming faith.
I remember well a conversation with Christians who were
canvassing my neighborhood with tracts on salvation, seeking

converts. As I invited them in and we talked, I was painfully aware that they were not interested in me, in knowing me, or in hearing about God's work in my life. They were intent on saving a soul, and this could only be done by fulfilling their step-by-step process. The fact that I was a follower of Jesus and belonged to a church was not sufficient for them. Yet I also remember wondering inside, "Am I any more welcoming in my faith than they are? Am I more interested in my welcoming shtick than in knowing and loving the person who stands before me?" Now when I approach a newcomer at church, I am determined not to repeat what I experienced with the Christians at my door.

The experience of unwelcome was reinforced recently by a friend who left the church years ago. He said that now, when he read stories about Christians in the news — in this case, Christians lobbying against gay marriage — he was more convinced than ever that churchgoers are more interested in being right than in welcoming others. Ouch!

For one young couple, unwelcome was disguised by initial friendliness. Jeff and Hillary were very impressed on their first visit to First United Church of Christ (UCC). They were greeted warmly at the door, given information about the church, and shown to the sanctuary. The next week, they were greeted again, this time by someone else, given information about the church, and shown to the sanctuary. The third visit, they declined the church information again, knew where the sanctuary was, and seated themselves. The greeting was stellar, but hospitality ended there. Friendliness is an important part of hospitality. But if we stay at the Wal-Mart greeter stage, hospitality will not take root. Jeff and Hillary wondered how to make friends in the church, how to move more deeply into the congregation's life. They were spiritually hungry, but their initial enthusiasm waned as week after week passed without any connecting. They stopped coming to church and no one noticed. As a Christian family, we are convicted by the damage done in these all too real experiences of unwelcome. At stake is the gospel food of God's welcome.

Indeed, at stake is the good news itself. When we fail to make plain God's welcome in salvation, we easily misrepresent God and the nature of salvation to the world. In effect, we don't tell the truth about who God is, the God who welcomes and cherishes, the God who longs to save. Christianity has come dangerously close in recent generations to squandering the truth of the gospel by presenting the God of Stan's childhood to the world. This is neither biblical nor faithful. We must be witnesses through our lives and voices to the God who welcomes. When we fail to proclaim God's welcome, we leave doors closed, we turn those hungry for welcome away unfed, squandering the gospel and breaking God's heart.

Our practices of hospitality begin with friendliness, and extend into the very depths of our lives. So many who have been alienated by Christian teaching are hungry for abundant, eternal life, for God's own life. We, the Christian family, can extend God's welcome through hospitality and welcome them all home.

Chapter 2

God's Welcome

Welcome is a basic human experience, and it comes in all shapes and sizes. Think of the welcome given by Wal-Mart greeters or the brief greeting when you come home from work. Think of the welcome upon returning to your childhood home or being received into your spouse's family. Some welcomes are more deliberate than others. How does God's welcome fit into our many experiences of welcome?

Two Welcomes

Jesus begins a story of two lost sons, "There was a man who had two sons..." (Luke 15:11–32). One cashes in on his inheritance and squanders all he has received through his own arrogance and pride. The other son is lost in his own dutifulness, and he too squanders all he has received through his own arrogance and pride. The father welcomes home the wandering son with open arms, running to meet him and wrapping him in the best cloak. The father welcomes the elder, dutiful son with the invitation to celebration, saying, "My son, you are always with me, and all I have is yours." Two sons. Two welcomes.

For some of us, God's welcome has come as it did to the younger son — only after we have wandered in a far country, seeking the things we thought we wanted, but finding our hands empty and our hearts broken. Anne Lamott tells of her own wandering in alcohol and drugs, a country so consuming

31

she could not remember any other. Her first, tentative steps out of that country were like following a distant chorus, barely audible, and took her into a small, ragtag congregation.

> When I went back to church, I was so hung over that I couldn't stand up for the songs, and this time I stayed for the sermon, which I just thought was so ridiculous, like someone trying to convince me of the existence of extraterrestrials, but the last song was so deep and raw and pure that I could not escape. It was as if the people were singing in between the notes, weeping and joyful at the same time, and I felt like their voices or *something* was rocking me in its bosom, holding me like a scared kid....I took a long deep breath and said out loud, "All right. You can come in." So this was my beautiful moment of conversion.[1]

The story doesn't end there. Lamott finds God's welcome occurring again and again as she struggles to quit drinking, as she raises her son, as she faces her own narcissism and self-loathing. Lamott's record of God's welcome — experienced in mercy, grace, and patience, this "*something* . . . rocking me in its bosom, holding me like a scared kid" — sounds a lot like the father in Jesus' parable. We may not all have such a dramatic conversion story, but we know what it's like to be lost and then found. We get lost in estrangement with a family member and find our way to reconciliation. We get lost in status seeking and get found in simple play with our children. We get lost in trying to live up to others' expectations and get found in discovering our true vocation.

For others of us, God offers the kind of welcome the elder son got. Maybe you have known God's welcome from the very beginning of your life. You did not have to wander in a far

---

1. Anne Lamott, *Traveling Mercies: Some Thoughts on Faith* (New York: Anchor Books, 1999), 50.

country first. You may feel like the older brother: Why do the Anne Lamotts of the world get all the attention? Here we are, going to church, living faithfully as best we can, trying to follow Jesus, loving God and neighbor. No one ever threw us a party or published a book about us. God's welcome in this case is a wake-up call: we have had abundant life all along! This welcome penetrates our hard-heartedness, as it did the elder son's, to remind us, "you are always with me, and all I have is yours." God's welcome is an invitation to the party God is throwing, an invitation to celebrate God's lavish generosity for both sons.

God's Welcome

In the parable of the two welcomes, God's reception is ready and waiting. Often we think of God as the prize at the end of an obstacle course. Instead, Scripture tells us that God's welcome is as close as our own breath. Right here, right now. In fact, the father in the parable is downright impatient, calling for the robe and ring to be brought before the repentant son can even finish his planned speech. Henri Nouwen, in his reflection on this parable, says,

> For most of my life I have struggled to find God, to know God, to love God....Now I wonder whether I have sufficiently realized that during all this time God has been trying to find me, to know me, and to love me....The question is not, "How am I to love God?" but "How am I to let myself be loved by God?" God is looking into the distance for me, trying to find me, and longing to bring me home.[2]

---

2. Henri Nouwen, *The Return of the Prodigal Son: A Story of Homecoming* (New York: Doubleday, 1992), 106.

God's ready welcome seeks *us*. We might ask Nouwen's question this way: How am I to let myself be welcomed by God?

God's welcome is neither partial nor tentative. In this parable, Jesus tells of a father who welcomes wholeheartedly, withholding nothing. We might expect a wronged parent to delay the party until after the wayward child has completed a rehab program and proves he can show up for work on time. Instead, this father offers the best he has, the fatted calf, the finest robe, the family ring. We might even judge the father as being a bit too extravagant, even wasteful, with his gifts. Yet no hint is given here of conditional welcome.

The words of the father's welcome to the elder son are even more stunning, "All that is mine is yours." All. A welcome deep and wide. A welcome complete. Here we might expect the father to scold the elder son into generosity. Instead, the father's own melted heart is expressed, and he offers all he has to his son.

If Jesus' story is the template of God's welcome, our lives are full of the prints it has made. We have known God's welcome in recovery from addiction, in forgiving one who has hurt us, in the new perspectives gained from a mission trip. Like the younger son, we have been lost and then we have been found. Like the elder son, we have been awakened to God's presence, living in us all along.

God's Welcome in the Bible

In the story of the welcoming parent, we get a glimpse of God's M.O. (*modus operandi,* or way or working). The Bible is full of stories about how God's welcome shows up. Here are a few:

◆ Genesis 18: We've already seen Abraham and Sarah welcome three strange travelers under the oaks of Mamre only to discover that these apparent strangers offer God's own welcome into a whole new life of parenthood and into the fulfillment of God's promise. In gospel hospitality, strangers often bear God's welcome.

◆ Joshua 2, 6: Rahab, the outsider, a non-Israelite and prostitute to boot, is the host offering hospitality to Joshua's spies in Jericho, ensuring the victory of God's people in the promised land (Josh. 2). Later, Rahab and her family are given sanctuary as Jericho is taken (Josh. 6). In gospel hospitality, hosts become guests and guests become hosts.

◆ Ruth: The story of Ruth and Naomi depicts two women, both widows, both outsiders by all accounts, whose lives seem destined for tragedy. Ruth, Naomi's daughter-in-law, refuses this death-in-life and invites herself to journey along with Naomi — where you go, I will go (Ruth 1:16) — welcoming Naomi into a different future than either of them could have imagined. As it turns out, a series of welcomes unfolds. Ruth and Naomi are welcomed into Boaz's house, and all three of them welcome the birth of a child, who will become the grandfather of King David. In gospel hospitality, welcomes unfold, one upon another.

◆ 1 Kings 17: The widow of Zarephath offers hospitality to the prophet Elijah, though she and her son are on the verge of starvation themselves (1 Kings 17). Her risky hospitality issues in miraculous abundance whereby they are all fed from a bottomless jar of meal and jug of oil. In gospel hospitality, meager resources bravely shared turn scarcity into abundance.

- God welcomes the wayward Israelites back into covenant again and again throughout the Hebrew Bible. God's hospitality is not predicated upon our faithfulness or obedience (Joshua, Judges, 1 and 2 Samuel, 1 and 2 Kings).

- Matthew 22, Luke 14: Jesus tells the story of the house-holder who threw a party for his friends, but when the regulars didn't show, he sent his servants to the streets to welcome everyone else to the party. God's hospitality extends beyond the usual guest list to the unlikely guests, welcomed to the party.

- Matthew 4, Mark 1, Luke 5: In the Gospels, Jesus proclaims the good news of God's welcome and calls fishermen from their nets, welcoming them into a radical ministry where they too welcome others into kingdom lives of healed bodies and restored spirits. God's M.O. shows that one welcome leads to a whole new life.

- In another story, Jesus enters a Samaritan town as a stranger and is welcomed by a woman at the well, only to become the host himself, offering her living water (John 4). Jesus' preaching and healing demonstrate that God's welcome cannot be constrained by age, status, illness, sex, wealth, or sin. Jesus' own ministry and teaching is grounded in the radical character of God's hospitality. He intentionally seeks "the lost sheep of the house of Israel" (Matt. 15), those outside the community of faith, the ritually and socially unclean, the sick, the demon-possessed (Matt. 10:5–8), proclaiming to them the nearness of God's realm, God's welcome. Jesus welcomes all these outsiders into God's life. His ministry is defined by this welcome, and ours is also: "The Spirit of the Lord is upon me, because he has anointed me to bring good news to the poor. He has sent me to proclaim release to the captives and recovery of sight to the blind, to let the oppressed go free, to proclaim the year of the Lord's favor" (Luke 4:18–19).

- Matthew 25: Also in the Gospels, Jesus connects welcoming strangers to welcoming Jesus himself. In the story of the separation of the sheep and the goats, he claims, "I was hungry and you gave me food. I was thirsty and you gave me something to drink. I was a stranger and you welcomed me. . . . Just as you do it for whoever is the least of these in my family, you do it to me" (Matt. 25). In gospel hospitality, welcoming strangers is equivalent to welcoming Christ himself.

Hospitality is at the very heart of the good news revealed in Scripture. Like the father in the previous story of the two lost sons, God's welcome is ready and eager throughout the Bible. God's welcome shows up as hosts become guests and guests become hosts, the welcome always coming full circle. God welcomes through outsiders and the lowly. God welcomes those who reject the invitation as well as those who simply fail to respond. God welcomes those who are distrustful as well as those who hope to gain advantage in the welcome. God welcomes the tentative as well as the confident. God's welcome reveals miraculous abundance. God's welcome calls people into new lives. God's welcome is extravagant, expansive, prodigal.

God's Welcome in Our Everyday Lives[3]

Just as God's welcome shows up in the lives of men and women in Scripture, so God's welcome shows up in our lives. Not one time only, but over and over. We usually identify it as grace, forgiveness, or mercy. But we also experience it

---

3. Stories are composite accounts with names changed for anonymity.

in creativity, friendship, and challenge. God's welcome happens every day, in big and small ways. There is no place in our lives that God is not at work, welcoming us into abundant life. Jesus says it again and again, "The reign of God is near!" We might translate it, "God's welcome is right here!" We can live in God's welcome, not just at church, not just in Bible study, but in our everyday lives, in work and play, in joy and sorrow. God's welcome is, at its base, our experience of God's grace, pulling us ever deeper into God's own life. I like the way Eugene Peterson translates Paul's description of God's welcome in the second letter to the Corinthians: God welcomes us into "a wide-open, spacious life" (2 Cor. 6:11), a truly abundant life.

Think for a minute about the first experience of welcome you received in your current church family, maybe a warm smile and greeting on a Sunday morning. Probably your first experience of welcome conveyed to you an open, friendly spirit at this church. If not, it may have been your third or fourth visit at this church before you experienced welcome. Now remember the welcome you received the first time you really shared something personal in a small group, maybe a Sunday school class or Bible study. That was a deeper welcome, a welcome of your thoughts and struggles, a welcome of your faith journey. Now remember the welcome you received when you were in need during an illness or a crisis, and your church family reached out. This welcome, when your life was coming apart, may have been the deepest welcome of all.

God's welcome isn't always warm and fuzzy. Often we become aware of God's welcome when our lives are painful. The marks of gospel hospitality — readiness, risk, repentance, and recognition — have already clued us in to the way God's welcome disrupts and transforms us. The stories below describe the range of ways God opens doors of welcome into God's life.

Through forgiveness, challenge, disruption, even through illness and recovery. These are examples only, and you will think of lots more.

God's welcome through forgiveness

For many of us, the forgiveness we receive from someone we have hurt provides the most ready example of God's welcome in our lives. Or, more miraculous still, our own forgiveness of someone who has hurt us may provide that example. Being forgiven, or being able to forgive, welcomes us into abundant life, a "wide-open, spacious life."

Bud Welch tells his story of forgiveness to whoever will listen. His daughter, Julie, was killed in the Oklahoma City bombing. The light of his life, a bright, twenty-three-year-old woman, was taken from him in a flash on April 19, 1995. After almost a year of self-medicating with alcohol, Bud says, "I had to do something different because what I was doing wasn't working." He realized it was hatred and revenge that had led Timothy McVeigh to kill 168 people in the Murrah Federal Building that day. Early on, Bud says, "I wanted him to fry. In fact, I'd have killed him myself if I'd had the chance." Bud wondered how he could avoid falling prey to the same desire for vengeance that motivated his daughter's killer. He knew that Timothy McVeigh's execution might meet his desire for revenge, but never meet his need for restoration.

Over time, Bud came to forgive Timothy McVeigh, "a release for me rather than for him," and even went to visit McVeigh's father, Bill. Bud and others in the Forgiveness Project (*www.theforgivenessproject.com*) are quick to remind us that "forgiveness is a journey. You can forgive today and still feel the pain tomorrow." Forgiveness is no magic wand. For Bud, God's welcome opened the door into a life where he didn't keep score anymore, "a wide-open, spacious life." God's welcome rippled out.

God's welcome through challenge or change

Tom had worked for Allied Steel for fifteen years, working his way up to floor supervisor in fabrication and then to manager. He received consistently good evaluations from his superiors and had good health care and pension benefits. He was active in the community, at church, and in his kids' sports activities. When he was laid off without warning, he was angry: "Why is this happening to me? I've played by the rules, had a solid work ethic, been a good husband and father. This isn't fair!" The anger quickly turned to panic: "Will I be able to get another job and support my family? Will others see me as a failure? How can others respect me when I can't even respect myself?"

The next thirteen months were long and painful. Around the third month, Tom stopped waiting for his old boss to call and looked into a new training program at the community college. The biggest step came when he shared with some of the men in his Sunday school class just how few prospects there seemed to be for him out there. He hated asking for help, which felt like another failure, but Tom asked them to send job leads his way.

He came to see that he could not do this alone. In fact, this upheaval in his life helped him see that he had never been doing it alone. The more he networked with others, the more he could see the way others had been with him all along, supporting and making his work possible. Tom did get another job, though not as soon as he'd have liked. He learned that his worth as a child of God didn't depend on his employment. Most importantly, he realized his fear of failure had blocked his connection to God. He was really excited about learning new skills, even at forty-four. God welcomed him into new life.

God's welcome through disruption

God's welcome often shakes us up, disrupting our lives. Bill and Mary adored their son, Ryan. They were proud of his accomplishments in track and field and pleased to see him coming into his own in college. He had even secured a summer internship that would position him in his chosen field. His short time at home before starting the summer internship had been full of connecting and conversation, but the bombshell he dropped shattered their picture of Ryan's future — and of their own. Looking them full in the face, Ryan said he was gay and that, after years of confusion and wondering, he was ready to include his parents with him on this journey. Bill and Mary loved Ryan, and that wouldn't change, but this was not the future they had planned. God invited them into a different future, one they felt less prepared to enter, and for which they had no map.

God's welcome disrupted their lives, but — and here's the crazy thing — it also led them into abundant life. They leaned on their church family. They found a deeper trust in the love they had for each other and in God's love for all of them. They met other parents in a PFLAG (Parents and Friends of Lesbians and Gays) support group, and discovered the amazing love and support of other parents who knew their struggles and joys and would walk with them. While the surface of their lives didn't change all that much, the depth of their lives did.

For Doug, the disruption came when all he thought he knew about God was called into question. When he was diagnosed with stage 3 cancer, he felt betrayed by God. Doug had worked hard to live a life pleasing to God. He went to church, served as a deacon there, volunteered at the local soup kitchen, prayed regularly, and tried to follow Scripture. Wouldn't his obedience be rewarded with blessing? What sort of God was this, who allowed a faithful servant to get cancer?

Doug thought he had been doing the right thing, living his life this way, and now it was clear to him that God didn't play fair. For the first couple of weeks, he was too confused and stunned to talk about it, but then he got angrier and angrier.

Finally, one day he just exploded and really let God have it. He was surprised at himself and realized his outburst had probably been his most honest conversation with God to date. That began a whole new relationship to God. As he moved through treatment, he had to let go of much he had thought he believed about God — that God rewarded good people and punished bad, that God expected him to live by the rules in order to maintain a relationship with God, that his suffering showed God had abandoned him. Now Doug says that cancer was the doorway into a new life, where God welcomed him into a new relationship, a new understanding of God and God's work in his life. Doug discovered that God loves him like a father loves his child, 24/7, not just when he obeys. He came to know God's presence, not just in formal prayer or Scripture study, but in the chemo chair and the doctor's waiting room, in the nausea and wakeful nights, in the nurses and the support group. This was a God so much more powerful and present than he had ever known, a God more available who does not abandon the suffering, and he was grateful for this discovery. In an odd way, the disruption of cancer had forced Doug to lose so much of his life and yet gain so much real life, in God. A welcome into abundant life.

God's welcome through being broken open and recovering

For Kathy, God's welcome came as she entered her first AA meeting. She had feared others knowing her shame for a long time. Since she could remember, Kathy had always met others' expectations, wanting to please, and she had been success-ful — but at a terrible price. She felt lost in her own life, unable to keep up with the demands from those around her at work and at home. Alcohol kept her numb and functional. She was shocked when her doctor warned her that, at age thirty-eight, her liver was damaged and cirrhosis was setting in. Who would she be without alcohol? She didn't know if she could keep up appearances. Without alcohol, she feared her true self would be revealed, to the disappointment of everyone around her.

At her first AA meeting, Kathy heard others express similar fears, thoughts that had nagged at her for years just below the surface of consciousness, but which she had never voiced out loud. "I'm tired of living a lie. I can't do this anymore. I can't do this alone." Even as fear consumed her, relief flooded at the thought of laying down this heavy load, this burden of being perfect, of always having her act together, of always meeting others' expectations and being whoever they needed her to be.

At AA, Kathy learned that she wasn't perfect and that, in fact, she was powerless. This was good news! It wasn't on her shoulders anymore. She could lay it down. Give it to God. Sarah stood under the oaks of Mamre, too long childless, and laughed at the idea that God could welcome her out of resignation and into new life (Gen. 18). Kathy too was incredulous that life could be any different, but she responded to God's welcome into abundant life again and again each day on the long road of recovery.

God's welcome through a call to something new or risky

Anna had been in ministry for five years when she received a visit from her conference director. "What do you mean I'm going to start a new church?" Anna blurted out. "I've never even been a senior pastor. I know nothing about new church starts!" Hank looked at her levelly and calmly said, "Well, actually, you aren't starting the new church. God is. This new church will be born by the power of the Holy Spirit. God is doing amazing things." The rest of the day Anna listened to all the voices competing in her head. "Can I do this? Can God do this? I can't do this!"

Looking back over her life, Anna acknowledged that many amazing things had happened, and she could say that God was present in all of them — the call to leave the law firm and go to seminary, the opportunity to work with homeless women as they rebuilt their lives, this loving congregation that welcomed her husband and children. God's welcome had come before in all these ways, and now, she, the unlikeliest of women, was called to an unknown path. Can she receive this call? Can she meet God's welcome with her own? God's welcome is risky business.

God's welcome through reaching out of others

Bill tells about God's welcome in the kindness and comfort of others following a death in his family. Church members came over, asking if there were particular foods the family would like prepared. Of course! Living in the South, the family knew what foods would offer comfort: cheese grits casserole, homegrown sliced beef tomatoes, sweet potato pie, and fried okra. Bill said he hadn't thought about rituals surrounding funerals as part of hospitality before. Yet these simple gestures were what brought home God's welcome in the midst of loss.

God's welcome through second chances

I was blessed with many experiences of God's welcoming grace as a child, primarily from parents who conveyed to me that, no matter what, I was loved. I remember especially that phone call to tell my parents that, at sixteen years old, just three weeks after receiving my driver's license, I had been responsible for a car wreck. After initial assurances that I and the other driver were okay, my father said something remarkable to me over the phone. "Amy, I want you to get back in that car and drive. You are a good driver, and I don't want you to lose any confidence in yourself." What a moment of grace! Where he could have seen only failure or irresponsibility, my father instead saw beyond the accident to the person both he and I wanted me to be — a safe, confident driver. In that moment, like the younger son in Jesus' parable (Luke 15:11–32), I heard God's welcome, the one that calls to new life and fresh starts. The welcome from God that says, "You can do it," "I trust you," or, "No matter what, I love you."

God's welcome through awakening

Helen tells her story of awakening this way. When she first became part of the state committee for history in her denomination, the committee meetings were held in the library of a large downtown church. The officers sat around the big table and all the other committee members sat in folding chairs that were lined up, classroom style, behind the table. All the officers were white, but there were several African American committee members, all of whom were steered to the folding chairs. Helen encouraged Marie, one of the black members, to take a seat at the table. No sitting in the back of the bus in this venue! Marie agreed immediately and chose a seat at the table. The staff director protested, but Marie did not give up her seat.

After the meeting, Henry, a longtime officer in the group, came to Marie to ask her forgiveness. It had never occurred to him before Marie sat at the "big table" that what they'd long done was racist, but as soon as he saw her sitting there, he realized their sin. It was a real eye-opening experience for him. No big fuss, no hysterics, just the simple matter of Marie quietly insisting that she sit at the table had made him aware of how wrong they — he — had been.

It took several more meetings, but Helen says she and Marie were finally able to convince the committee to change their seating arrangements. They ended up moving the meetings to another room, where everyone could sit around the table. No surprise: it changed the entire tenor of the meetings. Committee members became much more participatory and a number of African American members were persuaded not only to accept positions on the committee but also to take leadership roles. The invisible became visible as God's welcome awakened Helen and the entire committee to racial issues in ways they had not seen.

Do these stories ring any bells for you? How have you known God's welcome in your life? Your story of God's welcome is particular to your life. These stories, as well as your own, bear the spiritual marks of gospel hospitality. Bud Welch's forgiveness came only when his heart was ready. Mary and Bill risked walking into a new future with their son, Ryan. Kathy's life was decentered and turned as God welcomed her into recovery from addiction. Tom learned to recognize his true value as a child of God. Gospel hospitality grows in this soil of our lives. From these experiences of God's welcome, we can then welcome others.

God's Welcome in Our Church Families

The welcomes from God to abundant life we experience in our individual lives have parallels in our congregational lives. We can think of similar accounts of grace, challenge, disruption, risk, and forgiveness in our congregations. Some of our church families have, like the younger son in the parable of the lost sons, experienced God's welcome after a great crisis where we have lost our way. Other congregations have known God's welcome as the older brother, hearing God's reminder, "I am always with you. Everything I have is yours."

God's welcome through change

Many churches have been through the deep disappointment and disruption of losing core members, often because local economies and jobs have shifted. In the midst of such disruption, many have had to do some radical re-visioning of their church's mission. Not unlike Tom, who lost his job and had to re-vision his life, many congregations have found God's welcome to abundant life came through crisis and disruption. For many congregations, God's welcome is marked by risk and repentance or turning. We live in God's welcome as a church family when we struggle through any kind of change — a change in pastors or staff, a change in the configuration of space or even the change of growing membership. Watershed experiences of change, whether we experience them positively or negatively, are part of the landscape of God's welcome. In each struggle, God welcomes us as God "does a new thing."

God's welcome through different heritages

Another common experience of God's welcome arises when members have different ritual and theological traditions. These differences often first present themselves as a rub or even clash when we try to organize our life together. Those who grew up in "Bible churches" want more explicit teaching on Scripture from the pulpit, while those from "high church" traditions may want to celebrate communion weekly. More often, however, the tensions are much less explicit because they are rooted in traditions and practices at the edges of our awareness.

These differences are regions in the landscape of God's welcome that we often avoid or find uncomfortable. God is at work in these differences, welcoming us into the larger Christian family, where differing practices and theologies all make up the full body of Christ. Some have started to speak of "theological hospitality" as a way to live together within our theological and denominational differences. Through theological hospitality, we acknowledge God's welcome by welcoming one another within the Christian family and the particular gifts God offers in the various traditions and practices we each bring.[4]

A parking lot for workers

For a church in a large city's suburb, God's welcome was revealed through painful struggle. Some day laborers gathered in their church parking lot early one morning, waiting for contractors to stop to hire them. Because the church sat on a main thoroughfare, its parking lot was a logical location for contractors looking for day workers. Church members had ignored it at first because the men gathered at dawn in the church's parking lot over on the edge, next to the convenience store where they could buy coffee. But as their ranks grew, sometimes more than fifty men, most of them immigrants, would mill around in loose groups, filling more and more of the church property. Those who weren't chosen early would stay through the day in hope of getting work.

Joe, the pastor, knew that most of the men there struggled to support their families. He'd heard of more than one incident where one of the men had been dropped off at the end of the day without pay. Worse were the accounts of injuries on the job. Still, the men would be there again the next morning, even with the risks involved.

---

4. For example, see W. David Buschart, *Exploring Protestant Traditions: An Invitation to Theological Hospitality* (Downers Grove, Ill.: InterVarsity Press, 2006), and Richard J. Foster, *Streams of Living Water: Celebrating the Great Traditions of the Christian Faith* (San Francisco: HarperSanFrancisco, 1998).

Phil had been a church member for more than twenty years and was truly distressed by the brewing conflict in the church over the situation. Phil heard the chatter. "This is private property after all, and it belongs to us." "If they don't have proper ID, then they don't belong here." Some members became outraged when they realized that the men left trash and even urinated by the trees at the back of the lot because they had no toilet facilities. "They're invading our space." Some church members wanted the police to take care of it and simply arrest them for trespassing. Other church members wanted the church to help the men find permanent employment, another way to get them out of the lot. Still others said, "Our church belongs to God, not to us," or "Why don't we let them use the church bathrooms?"

On top of the internal reactions, the surrounding businesses and neighbors approached the church about putting a stop to the day laborers congregating in the parking lot. They said it was bad for business and endangered children going to school. As chairperson of the church council, Phil was concerned about the church property, but he was also concerned that the church provide a faithful response. It was clear the church would have to act. But how? Was this a property issue for the trustees to deal with? Was this a political issue about immigrant rights on which to make a public stand? What was God calling them to do?

Phil talked to the pastor in preparation for the council's discussion of the issue. He knew there were strong feelings among some church leaders to take legal action against the men. As they thought about a Scripture passage that might ground the discussion, the pastor suggested Matthew 25, Jesus' words, "I was a stranger and you welcomed me." Phil immediately resonated. "I know we will have to address the property and political issues here, but I want to reframe the conversation first. God is presenting us with an opportunity

to participate in hospitality." In that night's discussion, there
was plenty of prayer, disagreement, and discernment about
what God was calling them to do.

Phil began by asking folks to tell stories of times they
had been strangers and were welcomed. They talked about
welcoming strangers and about how they had known God's
welcome in their own lives. As people told stories of their
own welcome, they also began to talk about their mission as a
congregation. Their mission statement declared, "We are followers of Jesus Christ, who reveals God's love to the world"
and "We are commited to sharing our faith through love lo-
cally and globally." They also pointed to the "open minds,
open hearts, open doors" banner on their church building,
more than just a slogan. As they talked, they began to see the
men in the parking lot through the eyes of God's welcome.
The meeting ended with all agreeing to pray further and see
where God might lead them.

Some church members began serving coffee to the men
in the church parking lot, introducing themselves and greeting them. The church council knew that extending God's
welcome to strangers meant inviting the men to be in the
conversation, to be part of the solution. They eventually set
up a task force to address issues together, including the pastor, church members, day laborers, the chief of police, and the
mayor. Paying attention to God's welcome in their own lives
and in their congregation didn't provide an easy answer to the
very complicated issue before them, but it set the landscape
for conversation and discernment. Connecting the ways God
had welcomed them to the ways they might welcome others
shifted the conversation from how to solve the problem of day
laborers in the parking lot to how to be faithful to God's call
to hospitality.

God's welcome in the ordinary

We also experience God's welcome as congregations in more mundane, everyday ways in our life together. Recently, a friend at church, Kevin, commented at a church supper, "Wow. Just stop and look around. All this noise and energy — God's people in fellowship and celebration." His simple recognition of our life together pointed to God's welcome. Congregations experience God's welcome when they experiment with worship or plan a mission trip. We experience God's welcome when the youth group holds a car wash or helps teach Vacation Bible School. God's welcome is present in every aspect of our lives together.

Welcomed into What?

To say that we are welcomed into God's life may sound abstract, as though we are being taken up into the clouds, because we often image God living somewhere far away. So what does it mean to be welcomed into God's life? The simplest answer is that to be welcomed into God's life is to be welcomed into abundant life, the deep, true place where God's reign is made manifest. Jesus calls this place the kingdom of God.

The biblical witness gives us some glimpses, as the stories above remind us. God's welcome calls people into new ways of being, seeing, and living, into abundant life. Sarah and Abraham are welcomed into incredulous parenthood in their old age. The Israelites are welcomed into the wilderness. The woman at the well is welcomed into the truth about her life. The blind and lame are welcomed to the party. So much of the picture we get from the Bible about God's welcome is that it's seldom what we expect it to be. God's welcome doesn't look like success by the world's standards, or even by the church's standards, in some cases.

Yet for each of us, and for each of our congregations, our welcome into God's life is particular and concrete. We each have a story to tell. There's no formula of what it looks like to be welcomed into God's life. It is very different to be welcomed into a wilderness than to a party, yet both depict God's particular welcomes. Jesus calls it abundant life. Paul calls it "a wide-open, spacious life" in his second letter to the Corinthians (2 Cor. 6:11, THE MESSAGE).[5]

God welcomes us like the father in Jesus' parable of the two lost sons. God's welcome is eager and expectant and is not conditioned by our response. Scripture is full of accounts of God's welcome. We know this welcome in each of our lives, in a host of ways, and in our lives together as congregations. God welcomes us into abundant life, into eternal life, into God's own life.

5. Eugene H. Peterson, *The Message: The Bible in Contemporary Language* (Colorado Springs: NavPress, 2002).

Chapter 3

Practicing Gospel Hospitality

How do we live gospel hospitality in real life? Throughout the centuries, Christians have called the intentional and mindful living out of our faith "spirituality." Spirituality can sound fluffy or insubstantial, but in truth it is made up of concrete, everyday *practices* that pay attention to God. A spirituality of hospitality is the particular practice of *paying attention to God's welcome* in our lives and paying attention to the welcome we extend to others.

Spirituality of Hospitality: Paying Attention

When we talk about hospitality we usually think first of how we welcome others. To cultivate a spirituality of hospitality, we need to back up a bit, and focus first on God as the source of any welcome we offer. This shifts our attention slightly, reframing the starting place for hospitality. When we focus first on God's welcome, instead of our own, we begin to pay attention in new ways and to see God's welcoming work as our source.

The purpose of the concrete practices of Christian spirituality and, in this case, practices that develop a mindfulness of God's welcome, is to shape our hearts as well as our actions. God's welcome starts to become who we are, not just what we do. Paying attention helps us embody hospitality deep in our bones. By paying attention, we not only live in welcome. Gospel hospitality lives in us.

The desert mothers and fathers of the third century tell a story about paying attention. A novice asked the teacher, "Holy One, is there anything I can do to make myself closer to God?" The elder replied, "As little as you can do to make the sun rise in the morning." The novice responded, "Then of what use are these spiritual disciplines of prayer?" The teacher answered, "To make sure that you are awake when the sun rises."[1] Practices that pay attention to God's welcome keep us awake, so that we don't miss the opportunities for hospitality we encounter every day. We are distracted, burdened, unable to believe God's invitation is even there. Practices of paying attention help us see through the clutter of our lives to notice these daily welcomes.

Paying attention — or mindfulness or staying awake, all ways to talk about the spirituality of hospitality — is a lifelong journey, not a one-time event. We do not learn to embody welcome by reading the right book or hearing the right sermon or taking a course in hospitality, though all of these may help. Rather, gospel hospitality as a way of life emerges from the discipline of paying attention. Mindfulness of God's welcome, practiced over time, reorients our hearts toward love of God and neighbor, renewing the image of God in us (Matt. 22:37; Mark 12:30; Luke 10:27; 2 Cor. 3:18).

Cultivating a Spirituality of Hospitality: Experimental Meditations

Since spirituality means practices that pay attention to God's welcome, these meditations offer some first practical steps.

---

1. Adapted from Joan Chittister, *The Rule of Benedict: Insights for the Ages* (New York: Crossroad, 1992), 32.

Each meditation has four parts. Each begins with (1) a Scripture reading followed by (2) a reflection on that passage and the insights it holds for a spirituality of hospitality. Next, (3) questions to ponder create some open space to continue your own reflection or group discussion on the Scripture passage and issues presented. Finally, each meditation offers (4) an experiment to try in cultivating a spirituality of hospitality.

Meditation 1:
Paying Attention

Scripture: Mark 8:17b–18

Do you still not perceive or understand? Are your hearts hardened? Do you have eyes and fail to see? Do you have ears and fail to hear? And do you not remember? (NIV)

Reflection

Jesus questions whether his followers are actually paying attention, and his questions hit home for us today. Going through the course of a day, we put one foot in front of another, going from one thing to the next. We may not "see" or "hear" in the ways Jesus means here. In the numbing busy-ness of life, we may not "remember." When asked, each of us could recount the great blessings in our lives, the gifts we have received from God. But without such prompting most of us are not awake to God's welcome. Jesus calls this paying attention "having eyes to see and ears to hear."

We already know how to pay attention to the things we care about. We develop habits over time to exercise, pay bills, ask our children about their homework, or pray daily. A friend of mine was frustrated that, even when he wanted to pay attention, in this case by remembering his family members' birthdays, he didn't succeed. He heard about a company that he could pay to remind him a week before each birthday, or, for a few dollars more, he could pay them to actually send a gift on each birthday on his behalf. On the face of it, this looked like a great way to solve his problem. After a year, he realized that while his loved ones were receiving birthday gifts, ostensibly from him, he was still no better at remembering their birthdays. Changing the outcome — gift-giving — was relatively easy. Changing his interior was considerably harder.

My friend tried again, this time not by trying to remember birthdays at all. Instead, he taped a short, daily prayer of thanksgiving for his loved ones to his car visor so he would see it on his way to work: "I'm so grateful for Mary, David, and Drew." The first week, he noticed it only three days out of five. Though not great, that was better than before, and he gave thanks as often as he remembered to. After a few months, he was surprised that the short, daily remembrance had helped him start to notice other small, everyday things, like the way his eight-year-old son always told him when they got in the car, "Put your seatbelt on, Daddy," and that his brother ended his emails with the sign-off line, "your brother." Slowly, his consciousness was changing — though remembering birthdays was still out of his reach. The simple, daily remembrance cultivated a new awareness of those he loved, an interior space of gratitude.

In our congregational lives, too, it may be easier to make surface changes, like getting visitors to walk through our doors, than to pay attention to reorienting our hearts so that we see Christ in them. Jesus' questions remind us to keep it simple — just use your eyes to see and your ears to hear. Remember to pay attention.

Questions to Ponder

• What methods of paying attention have you already in-corporated into your life for things that are important to you?

• What practices do you or your church family already have to help you pay attention to God's welcome?

• What do you think would change about your life if you paid attention to God's welcome more regularly?

• What do you think would change about your church's life if the congregation paid attention to God's welcome more regularly?

Experiment

In her book *A Christian View of Hospitality: Expecting Surprises,* Michele Hershberger describes "The Forty-Day Experiment." She suggests forming a group of at least ten people, but an individual could try this as well. Hershberger advises participants to commit themselves to three things:

1. To pray this prayer every day for forty days: "Lord, please send me a hospitality opportunity today."

2. To journal their experiences daily.

3. To be willing to share some of their experiences with the other participants in a worship service at the end of the forty days.[2]

Alternate Experiment: Telling Times

Incorporate a short time of telling about God's welcome in your lives at the beginning of church council meetings. Plan to spend five to seven minutes responding to these questions:

---

2. Michele Hershberger, *A Christian View of Hospitality: Expecting Surprises* (Scottdale, Pa.: Herald Press, 1999).

+ Where has God's welcome been present in your life over
the last week?

+ Where have you seen God's welcome in our church family
over the last month?

There are no right or wrong answers. The "telling time" is
a simple way to practice paying attention, to cultivate this
spiritual discipline. The first few times may be mostly full of
silence. That's fine. Let people ponder. It's also fine to invite
one or two people to think about this ahead of time and
be the ones to break the ice. These "telling times" can be
incorporated into any church meeting, class, or worship.

Meditation 2:
Welcoming the Stranger Within

Scripture: Matthew 5:43–48

*You're familiar with the old written law, "Love your friend," and
its unwritten companion, "Hate your enemy." I'm challenging that.
I'm telling you to love your enemies. Let them bring out the best in
you, not the worst. When someone gives you a hard time, respond
with the energies of prayer, for then you are working out of your
true selves, your God-created selves. This is what God does. He
gives his best — the sun to warm and the rain to nourish — to
everyone, regardless: the good and bad, the nice and nasty. If all
you do is love the lovable, do you expect a bonus? Anybody can do
that. If you simply say hello to those who greet you, do you expect
a medal? Any run-of-the-mill sinner does that. In a word, what
I'm saying is, Grow up. You're kingdom subjects. Now live like it.
Live out your God-created identity. Live generously and graciously
toward others, the way God lives toward you.* (THE MESSAGE)

Reflection

The idea of having a stranger inside may in itself be strange to you. In this passage from Matthew, Jesus calls us to love the unlovable. This applies even to the unlovable parts of ourselves. When we stop and take stock, we see parts of ourselves that we appreciate and cherish, and other parts that we wish would disappear — but they keep showing up uninvited! We each have our own list of unlovable strangers inside: irritability, the need to please others, the insecurities that keep us awake at night, the drive to criticize or gossip that comes over us sometimes. We all have strangers within.

For years, I was frustrated and impatient with others, especially women, who were timid or hesitant to speak up. I rolled my eyes at their tentativeness when I was ready to charge forward. Why couldn't they be more assertive?

My impatience with others was mirrored inside my own heart, where I had no welcome for the fearful voice inside me when it tried to speak. I wasn't afraid of anything! I had never connected the two experiences — my intolerance of fear within me and my intolerance of fear in others — until a wise friend pointed it out. What would it be like, she asked, to befriend the stranger within who is sometimes unsure or afraid? What if I treated that fearful voice inside me like a stranger at my door, welcomed it, and listened to it? She suggested that this stranger within surely had things to teach me about myself, perhaps a fuller, truer picture that I would never see as long as I shut out this stranger.

Sure enough, as I welcomed this stranger within I learned to listen to my fears and determine which ones were wise and which ones were not. I learned a lot about my own pride, about my desire to appear strong, and about receiving my fears so that I could give them over to God's keeping. Welcoming this stranger within, as with all welcoming, brought me closer

to God. The decentering of perspective, repentance, that occurs with welcoming strangers happened in my own heart. I
could start to welcome the tentative voices in others.

Many of the great spiritual teachers have pointed out that
it is often easier to welcome strangers "out there" than to
welcome the strangers "in here." We are less tolerant, graceful,
or forgiving of the alien voices within ourselves. Yet God's
welcome asks us to welcome all the parts of ourselves. The
great Rabbi Zusya puts it this way: "In the coming world, they
will not ask me 'Why were you not Moses?' They will ask me,
'Why were you not Zusya?' "[3]

Gospel hospitality happens inside us — God's welcoming
work within. God has already welcomed all those alien parts
within us that embarrass us or that we reject. Welcoming the
stranger within doesn't mean that we like the stranger within,
or that we want to become that stranger. We may decide,
once we have welcomed the stranger within, to send it on
its way, but only after we have received the gift it brings.
Henri Nouwen, the great Christian spiritual teacher, describes
it this way:

> It is God himself who reveals to us the movement of our
> own spiritual life. It is not the movement from weak-
> ness to power, but the movement in which we become
> less and less fearful and defensive and more and more
> open to the other and his world, even when it leads to
> suffering and death.[4]

All strangers bring gifts. Once acknowledged and welcomed,
the stranger within brings us eventually into more abundant
life. Nouwen is right: interior hospitality may indeed take us

---

3. Martin Buber, *Tales of the Hasidim: The Early Masters* (New York: Schocken
Books, 1975), 251.
4. Henri Nouwen, *Reaching Out: The Three Movements of the Spiritual Life*
(Garden City, N.Y.: Doubleday, 1975).

through suffering and a death of sorts — the decentering and reframing of self — but it is a suffering and death that leads to new life.

Questions to Ponder

♦ Who are the strangers within you?

♦ What happens when they arrive? Do you welcome them, ignore them, or shoo them away?

♦ What do you gain by rejecting the stranger within?

♦ What do you risk by welcoming the stranger within?

Experiment

Write an imaginary dialogue between you and a stranger within. First, identify an aspect of yourself you do not welcome. Let this stranger have its say and respond with your own thoughts and feelings. This can also be done in a role play, asking someone else to play your part, while you provide the internal stranger's side of the dialogue. If you were the voice of the stranger within, what would you want to say? What would you want your host self to hear?

Meditation 3:
Welcoming Theological Strangers

Scripture: 1 Peter 3:8–9

Finally, all of you, have unity of spirit, sympathy, love for one another, a tender heart, and a humble mind. Do not repay evil for evil or abuse for abuse; but, on the contrary, repay with a blessing. It is for this that you were called — that you might inherit a blessing. (NRSV)

Reflection

What a powerful image — "a humble mind"! We more often think of a humble heart than a humble mind. This Scripture passage calls for an intellectual humility that requires us not to participate in the tit-for-tat debates, "repaying abuse for abuse," that too often pass for Christian conversation.

You've heard it, and may have even been part of it. Christians debating other religions or gay marriage or what evangelism should look like. These debates often rely on scoring points using Scripture to prove one is right. The goal is to one-up the other viewpoint in order to win. This is certainly the model of discourse portrayed in the larger culture across the media. It is a discourse that seeks power more than truth, heat more than light. From talk shows to news pundits, one-upmanship dominates public discourse and Christians seem to have adopted it too in order to appear to be right, to win. But as followers of Jesus, we have a much more radical and countercultural witness to make: we can refuse to participate in one-upmanship and model theological hospitality instead.

A humble mind doesn't require us to dumb down our faith or check our brains at the door. A humble mind might be contrasted to a puffed-up mind, one with no room left to welcome God or anyone else because it is so full of itself. A humble mind knows that it doesn't know everything, that it is needful of others and of God's saving work through others. A humble mind is the place within us that allows us to reach out in gospel hospitality to welcome the theological stranger. We have no room to welcome a guest when we are preoccupied with ourselves.

When we welcome theological strangers we do more than tolerate them, we get to know them. Gospel hospitality has "eyes to see" them as more than their set of beliefs or biblical interpretations. We recognize them as children of God, made in the image of God and precious in God's sight. With God's help, we may even be able to see Christ in the theological stranger. Readiness, risk, repentance, and recognition mark such a welcome — all characteristics one learns first in one's own experience of God's welcome. Hearing others, receiving others without trying to change them, fix them, or judge them, is a powerful witness of "otherliness." Welcoming the theological stranger therefore takes considerable discipline and courage.

An important caveat: offering hospitality to the theological stranger does not mean we must agree with that person's positions or that we abandon our own. Nor does gospel hospitality require us to avoid conflict. Quite the opposite: welcome is the first step of genuine engagement, and genuine engagement can lead to genuine disagreement. Without theological hospitality, we are left with unengaged tolerance or with posturing opposite viewpoints. When this happens, it is typically a sign that we are more concerned with being right (a spirit full of itself) than with understanding the differences that divide (a humble mind). Scripture gives us a powerful alternative to repaying "abuse for abuse:" a humble mind. "It is *for this* that you were called" (v. 9).

Questions to Ponder

- When was the last time you welcomed someone with different theological or moral views than yours? What happened?

- When has your church welcomed theological strangers? What happened?

- How do you usually react to people with views different from yours?

- Who among your friends and relatives are strangers to you because of their faith?

- To whom are you the theological stranger? How do you want to be welcomed?

Experiment

Using a humble mind in conversation. You can try this experiment with a family member, church friend, or co-worker. Next time you find yourself in a conversation with someone you know has political views differing from your own, experiment with hospitality. Say, "I truly want to understand your views on _____ ." Think of yourself as a host welcoming a guest into your home. Stick to these two invitations:

- Tell me more about how you arrived at your views about this.

- Tell me more about how it is important in your life right now.

Your job is simply to listen and clarify, not to debate, convince, or put forth your own views. One way to do this is from time to time to reflect back to them what you hear them saying. For example, "Okay, so for you, this question [of other religions] really came to a head when your sister married a Jewish man." This gives the "stranger" a chance to clarify or enhance your understanding, and allows you to check on whether you are getting it.

When you sense yourself tempted to debate or move away from these two invitations, come back to them. You will likely get something of that person's life story — an event, relationship, or experience that shaped their view of the world and of this issue. This is a valuable opportunity to know others better, to see the things they care about deeply and appreciate them, even if you don't share their values or commitments.

Five to ten minutes are usually sufficient to listen, clarify, and receive the other person's views. Remember, the goal is not to come to an agreement on the issue, but to grasp as fully as you can the other person's view, how they came to that view, and how it is important to them now. At the end of the conversation you will (probably) still genuinely disagree with them and that need not be diminished. It's fine to say, "We sure have different views on this. Thanks for helping me understand yours."

After the experiment, ask yourself: What was hard about it? What was surprising or unexpected? What did you learn about the other person? About yourself? About hospitality? About God? What was the blessing in this experience? What would you do differently next time?

Meditation 4:
Welcoming Political Strangers
(variation on Meditation 3)

Scripture: 1 Peter 3:8–9

Finally, all of you, have unity of spirit, sympathy, love for one another, a tender heart, and a humble mind. Do not repay evil for evil or abuse for abuse; but, on the contrary, repay with a blessing. It is for this that you were called — that you might inherit a blessing. (NRSV)

Reflection

Like theological hospitality, being hospitable to differing viewpoints is a powerful witness Christians can make in the political sphere, too. Having a humble mind is a pretty radical idea when it comes to our political convictions, but we can live a spirituality of hospitality in all spheres of life, including politics. People who have political views different from our own, even people we know well, may seem like strangers to us — alien, confusing, often unfathomable. We may wonder:

How can they hold that position? What kind of person would vote that way?

Here too we can pray for a humble mind that does not "repay abuse for abuse." As Christians, we could radically alter the landscape of political polarization in U.S. culture by re-framing political differences in terms of hospitality rather than debate. Hospitality allows us to see our political opponents not as enemies to be defeated, but as strangers to be welcomed. When we welcome ideological strangers we do more than tolerate them: we receive them, we recognize them as children of God, made in the image of God and precious in God's sight. With God's help, we may even be able to see Christ in the political stranger.

Just like theological hospitality, offering hospitality to polit-ical strangers does not mean we must agree with their political positions or that we abandon our own. Nor does gospel hospi-tality require us to avoid conflict. Quite the opposite: welcome is the first step of genuine engagement that can lead to gen-uine disagreement. Without political hospitality, we are left with unengaged tolerance or with posturing opposite view-points, often more concerned with being right (a spirit full of itself) than with understanding the differences that divide (a humble mind). Scripture gives us a powerful alternative to repaying "abuse for abuse:" a humble mind. "It is *for this* that you were called" (v. 9).

Questions to Ponder

+ When was the last time you welcomed a political stranger? What happened?

+ When was the last time your church welcomed a political stranger?

+ Who among your friends and relatives are strangers to you because of political views?

- What happens inside you when you welcome new ideas or a political stranger?

- To whom are you a political stranger? How do you want to be welcomed?

Experiment

Using a humble mind in conversation. You can try this experiment with a family member, church friend, or co-worker. Next time you find yourself in a conversation with someone that you know has political views differing from your own, experiment with hospitality. Say, "I truly want to understand your views on _____ [fill in the blank]." Think of yourself as a host welcoming a guest into your home. Stick to these two invitations:

1. Tell me more about how you got to your views about this.

2. Tell me more about how it is important in your life right now.

Your job is simply to listen and clarify, not to debate, convince or put forth your own views. One way to do this is to reflect back to them what you hear them say from time to time throughout the conversation. For example, "Okay, so for you, the whole question of homosexuality was not even on your radar until recent years, so it's been a really new challenge to think about." This gives the "stranger" a chance to clarify or enhance your understanding and gives you a check on whether you are getting it.

When you sense yourself tempted to debate or move away from these two invitations, come back to them. You will likely get something of that person's life story — an event, relationship or experience that shaped their view of the world and of this issue. This is a valuable opportunity to know others better, to see the things they care about deeply and appreciate them, even if you don't share their values or commitments.

It's generally good to give yourself no more than five to ten minutes to listen, clarify, and receive the other person's views. Remember, the goal is not to come to an agreement on the issue, but to grasp as fully as you can the other person's view, how they came to that view, and how it is important to them now. At the end of the conversation you will still genuinely disagree with them and that need not be diminished. It's fine to say, "We sure have different views on this. Thanks for helping me understand yours."

After the experiment, ask yourself: What was hard about it? What was surprising or unexpected? What did you learn about the other person? About yourself? About hospitality? About God? What was the blessing in this experience? What would you do differently next time?

Meditation 5: Welcoming New Ways

Scripture: Isaiah 43:18–19

Do not remember the former things, or consider the things of old. I am about to do a new thing; now it springs forth, do you not perceive it? I will make a way in the wilderness and rivers in the desert. (NRSV)

Reflection

We usually think of hospitality in terms of welcoming people, but we can apply hospitality to welcoming new ideas or new ways of doing things, too. New folks bring new ideas and that can be disruptive. As new church members are welcomed onto committees and ministry teams, they may suggest changing the way the stewardship campaign is run, or switching to a different church school curriculum. This can be hard when the new ideas are "not the way we've always done it" or threaten our most cherished congregational practices. Welcoming new ways of doing things doesn't mean we have to always agree and act on them, but it does mean we take them seriously in prayerful discernment.

Through new ideas and ways, God may be "doing a new thing" (v. 18). When we welcome these new ideas, we are momentarily decentered as a community, perhaps shaken from our stagnation. The disequilibrium can be disorienting, yet it creates an opening for us to turn onto a new path, where God "will make a way in the wilderness and rivers in the desert" (v. 19). Gospel hospitality requires risk and repentance/turning.

For example, in one congregation some young adults wanted to start a contemporary service, including an amplified praise band. Many members were concerned worship would no longer be the same and the traditional service would have to compete (both of which were true). For some, the initial response was that an alien element had entered the congregation and threatened our way of life. Through the lens of hospitality, the worship committee was able to cast the issue in terms of welcome: How can we welcome new worship practices into our congregation? And, just as important: How is God's welcome present in all of our worship practices? The conversation was still difficult but the tone and center shifted by being framed in terms of hospitality. The worship committee sought to welcome Christ in the stranger, in this case, in different worship practices. The welcoming continues, as they live into different worship practices and find a home in God there. One thing is now clear: they want to live in God's welcome.

Questions to Ponder

+ When was the last time you welcomed a new idea or way of doing things? What happened?

+ When was the last time your church welcomed a new idea or way of doing things?

+ What do we risk when we welcome new ideas or ways of doing things?

Experiment

Try this fun experiment as a family. Ask your children to set the table for dinner in any manner they choose. Let them know that this is an experiment for the whole family in "doing a new thing." Once they have set the table, welcome this "new way" by leaving it the way they present it. At dinner, talk about welcoming new things into your life: Is it hard to try new things? Why? Share examples from your own life. What have each of you learned from this experiment? What does it teach you about hospitality?

Meditation 6:
Saying Yes and Saying No:
The Limits of Hospitality

Scripture: Matthew 11:28–30

Are you tired? Worn out? Burned out on religion? Come to me. Get away with me and you'll recover your life. I'll show you how to take a real rest. Walk with me and work with me — watch how I do it. Learn the unforced rhythms of grace. I won't lay anything heavy or ill-fitting on you. Keep company with me and you'll learn to live freely and lightly. (THE MESSAGE)

Reflection

Is it ever acceptable to not extend hospitality or to say no? Aren't Christians supposed to give and give and give, no matter what? The short answer is yes, it is fine to say no. In fact, it is necessary. In the passage from Matthew, Jesus' questions hit us where we live — tired, burned out. Jesus invites us to rest in him, to "live freely and lightly."

In order to "learn the unforced rhythms of grace," we have to practice saying yes and saying no. We have to practice making choices about what we can and cannot do. Our congregation cannot do everything and be everything to everyone. While this sounds obvious, many of us live in the illusion that we can and, moreover, that God expects us to. That's why we feel burned out or even resentful when we overextend and overcommit, as individuals or as congregations. The greatest spiritual danger in never saying no is a chronic sense of failure which, in turn, separates us from God's welcome. A chronic sense of failure is not abundant life.

Jesus' invitation in the passage above is altogether different. He doesn't call us to do and be everything, but rather "to recover your lives" — to recover the deepest callings of our hearts, to uncover the clutter from our lives to reveal what matters most, particular to each of us. Jesus invites us to lay down the illusion that we can do it all and instead embrace saying yes and saying no: yes to this, no to that. I am not gifted or called in every ministry of the church. It is okay for me to say that I have gifts for music ministry, but not for working with small children. I have time to be a greeter Sunday morning, but not to be a sponsor at the youth lock-in.

In fact, only by saying yes and saying no can we live honestly in God's life. The truth is, we deceive others when we pretend we will meet all their expectations and needs. As humans, we live within the limits of finite humanity. Only

God gets to be *infinite*. Finitude is not failure. In fact, God blessed our finitude by becoming incarnate in human life in Jesus Christ. Ironically, honesty about our limits enables our welcome to be bigger and better, because an honest welcome comes from the truth of our center, not from the ragged edges of exhaustion.

Learning to recognize our limits — to say yes and to say no — applies not only to our time and energy but also to our identity. Sometimes we will say no in order to be honest with visitors about who we are. This is hard because we genuinely want to make everyone feel at home. It's easy to fall into a customer service model of ministry where the "customer is always right." Yet sometimes we will have strangers in our midst who are uncomfortable with our denominational or congregational identity. Some visitors may oppose having women in the pulpit or feel uncomfortable hearing references to Jesus. Does that mean we stop allowing women in the pulpit or stop talking about Jesus? Of course not. We can't stop being ourselves — that's exactly the gift God has given us to share. To "recover our lives" we cannot give away the things we most deeply care about. Hospitality will require us to say at times, "No, we can't do that because that is not who God has called us to be." In fact, the very commitments that express our identity, the mission with which God has gifted us, is what defines our welcome. Without those identity boundaries we have no authentic welcome to give. Gospel hospitality focuses on God's welcome, not on getting people to like us.

When is it acceptable to say no? We hit the limits of hospitality when we violate our identity or mission, as individuals and as congregations. Gospel welcome comes from the deep core of our lives in God, not from a vacated identity. Jesus invites us to "recover [our] lives" and "learn the unforced rhythms of grace."

Lastly, saying yes and saying no is something that we can help each other do in our lives together as Christians. We can ask one another, when accepting a new role or task: Is God calling you to this task? What will you lay down in order to pick this up? We can call each other "to live freely and lightly."

Questions to Ponder

* Do you say yes and say no? Why or why not?

* To what things do you need to say no in order to "recover your life"?

* What happens in your spirit and in your congregation when you run up against limits of time, energy, or identity? Does that feel like failure? Why or why not?

* As a church family, what practices of discernment do we have to determine when we can say yes and when we need to say no? How do we talk about our boundaries of identity?

Experiment

Begin practicing saying yes and saying no by discussing how you decided to participate in this group or committee. Did you go through discernment or prayer? What factors did you consider: time, energy, passion, others' expectations, God's calling? In order to say yes to this participation, to what did you say no or decide to lay down? As congregations, we can ask one another each time we take on a new role or task: Is this task part of God's welcome in your life? To what will you say no in order to say yes to this?

As an individual experiment, make a list of three or four commitments and activities in your life. For each item, reflect on your decision-making process. Did you go through discernment or prayer? What factors did you consider — time, energy, passion, others' expectations, God's calling?

Just asking these questions helps us begin to pay attention to the ways we say yes and say no.

Meditation 7:
Empty Space

Scripture: Philippians 2:4–8

Let each of you look not to your own interests, but to the interests of others. Let the same mind be in you that was in Christ Jesus, who, though he was in the form of God, did not regard equality with God as something to be exploited, but emptied himself, taking the form of a slave, being born in human likeness. And being found in human form, he humbled himself and became obedient to the point of death — even death on a cross. (NRSV)

Reflection

We usually associate hospitality with being full, not with being empty. As hosts, we want to be full of things to give our guests, not empty with nothing to give. Scripture invites us, however, to turn this equation on its head, to empty our full-to-the-max lives to create space for others and for God.

The passage from Philippians connects "the mind that was in Christ" with Jesus having "emptied himself." God's welcome involves emptying ourselves in order to experience the "wide-open, spacious life" in God. What might that look like?

We empty ourselves as we lay down the false images of who we think we are supposed to be or who others expect us to be. We empty ourselves as we let go of some of our images of God to make room for new ones. We empty ourselves as we give up the need to be right or to have it all figured out and prescribe the truth to others. We empty ourselves as we give up grievances that maintain our superiority or our list of accomplishments that gives us status. The Philippians passage describes this emptying as being humbled, even to the point of death.

In the Gospels, Jesus puts it this way: "Those who want to save their life will lose it, and those who lose their life for my sake will find it" (Matt. 15:25; cf. Mark 8:35; Luke 9:24; John 12:25). A radical openness accompanies life in God's welcome — abundant life — that creates empty space, space to welcome strangers, space where new voices can join the conversation. A well-known story describes a Zen master who, on the first visit from a new disciple, poured tea into his student's cup and kept pouring. As tea flowed over the sides of the cup, the student finally exclaimed, "Stop! It's full and can't hold anymore!" The Zen master replied, "Like this cup, you are full of your own opinions and speculations. You must first empty your cup in order to learn Zen."[5]

Emptying is necessary in our churches as well, both figuratively and concretely. I remember working at a church whose fellowship hall had, over the years, become cluttered with quite an assortment of odd furniture. Couches, tables, chairs, and decorative items had been donated or placed there, each with its own history and meaning (though no one could remember where the ceramic figurines had come from!). When the fellowship hall was built in the 1950s, the large space was used for weekly fellowship dinners. Every week the hall had been filled with people and activity. Over the years, furniture had taken up more and more space, so that now the fellowship dinners were reduced to two banquet tables at one end of the room. Interestingly, the membership had gotten smaller too so that the aging congregation could, in fact, all fit around those two tables.

Then a fascinating thing happened. After an enthusiastic summer vacation Bible school, a few neighborhood families

5. Paul Reps, comp., *Zen Flesh, Zen Bones* (Garden City, N.Y.: Anchor Books, 1961), 5.

visited the following Sunday, staying for the fellowship dinner. As more chairs were added to these two already full tables, it was clear that there was no room for new folks. They could squeeze in around the edges, but the filled space would need some emptying before new folks could comfortably be added. The existing members weren't sure they could empty the space to make room for more tables. Each piece of furniture represented a person, event, or memory that was important. Yet the welcome in their hearts for these new families gave them the strength to make those tough decisions.

That was just the beginning. When a young dad offered to help in the kitchen, the able women who had been serving fellowship dinners for decades shot up their eyebrows in question, and then assured him that they didn't need help, they had everything taken care of. Their well-oiled organizational machine for cranking out church dinners left no empty slots for helpers. Quickly sensing his disappointment, Betty regrouped, "Sure, you could put the bread out — the baskets are on top of the freezer."

Opening up spaces to include new people in our life together may require some of us to step aside or lay down a task so that someone else can pick it up. Philippians calls us to many kinds of emptying in order to welcome.

As we cultivate a spirituality of hospitality within our churches, we can think not only about what we have to offer visitors, but also about what empty space we can open up to make room for them. It's at least as important to receive others as it is to give things to them. It's not a bad thing to fill a visitor's hands with brochures, activity schedules, and descriptions of our Sunday school classes and mission trips. But in addition, we need empty space, like the unscheduled time between Sunday school and worship, not only to greet visitors, but also to listen to them, to receive their lives and the gifts they bring. Henri Nouwen describes it this way:

The paradox of hospitality is that it wants to create emptiness, not a fearful emptiness, but a friendly emptiness where strangers can enter and discover themselves as created free; free to sing their own songs, speak their own languages, dance their own dances; free also to leave and follow their own vocations. Hospitality is not a subtle invitation to adopt the life style of the host, but the gift of a chance for the guest to find his own.[6]

This "friendly, empty space" is a powerful place for God's welcome.

Questions to Ponder

• In what ways are you "full of yourself?" What in your life needs emptying?

• In what ways is your church family too full? What in the church's life needs emptying?

• Where are the "friendly, empty spaces" in your church's life?

Experiment

For an individual: Do an "empty space inventory" of one day of your life. Pick a day on your calendar and identify two times in the day when you have fifteen minutes of empty space, that is, time not scheduled with a commitment, chore, or other activity. If no empty space is apparent on your calendar, clear out a space you can reliably keep empty. For one day, protect each of these fifteen-minute time slots when you are tempted to fill it with a quick errand or phone call or TV. Leave that space empty. This may be hard because it can feel like unproductive time. That's okay. Experience fifteen minutes of empty space. Just breathe. Be fully present to where

---

6. Nouwen, *Reaching Out*, 72.

you are. Welcome the empty space, like you would a guest. See what happens, what thoughts emerge, or what opportunities present themselves. Discover what happens in empty space, whatever it is.

For a group: A Sunday school class, study group, or ministry committee can incorporate empty space into each meeting. Commit to incorporating empty space for six consecutive meetings. At the beginning of each gathering, open with a short prayer, followed by five minutes of silence. This empty space may be jarring for the first few times, but our Quaker brothers and sisters remind us of its value. At the end of the gathering (not at the end of the silence), take two minutes to discuss the experience of the empty space of silence and how it made a difference in the rest of your time together. Your observations on the difference that silence makes will change over the six sessions, so continue to check in at the end of each time. Silence is pretty threatening to most of us, so be gentle with yourselves and give up to God all expectations about it.

Modify: If five minutes feels too overwhelming, start with three minutes. By the fifth or sixth meeting, you may want to lengthen the silence to seven to ten minutes.

Meditation 8: Seeing Christ in the Stranger

Scripture: Matthew 25:35–36

I was hungry and you gave me food, I was thirsty and you gave me something to drink, I was a stranger and you welcomed me, I was naked and you gave me clothing, I was sick and you took care of me, I was in prison and you visited me.... Truly I tell you, just as you did it to one of the least of these who are members of my family, you did it to me. (NRSV)

Reflection

Jesus tells us in Matthew 25 that it is in the least likely of places — in prisons and sickbeds, among the hungry and thirsty, even among the lost — that we will encounter Jesus himself. His parable suggests that Jesus may be especially present among the vulnerable. If we want to know Jesus, we're going to have to hang out with strangers.

At first blush this seems counterintuitive. Wouldn't we want to hang out with models of Christian faith, maybe clergy or church leaders, if we want to know Jesus? Certainly we will seek out brothers and sisters who can offer their wisdom and faith as we journey along. But if we turn only to those sources to know Jesus, we will miss out on some of God's profound welcome. As we cultivate a spirituality of hospitality we want eyes to see Jesus in each person we encounter, even when the Jesus we find there is not the Jesus we expect.

You already know the experience of seeing Christ in another person. Most likely, you have experienced the grace of God's welcome into abundant life through another person in your life. As you reflect on those in whom you have encountered Jesus most profoundly, what was it that conveyed Christ's presence to you? Perhaps their gentleness, mercy, or forgiveness. Or perhaps their devotion to others or their holiness of life. It's not a big stretch to believe we can see Christ present in these ways. But how can we see Jesus in those who do not exhibit such likeable traits? How can we see Jesus in the talkative persons who interrupt and seem uninterested in anyone's thoughts but their own? Or in the perfectionist who seems to have little patience with others who don't measure up? Could we see Jesus in the panhandler on the sidewalk or in the shabbily dressed stranger who visits on Sunday morning, standoffish and shuffling to a seat?

To be fair, it takes time and patience to develop this spiritual discipline of seeing Jesus in others. For most of us, it doesn't come naturally. We have to desire this state of the heart, and it begins with trust. Trust that God is, indeed, pervading every molecule of the universe, so God must already be at work in this person, planting seeds, calling them to abundant life, nudging and welcoming them.

Notice: our trust is not in the goodness of the other person, or even in our own ability to see Christ in the other, but in God's life itself, present and powerful in all things. Cultivating a spirituality of hospitality pulls us back to this foundational trust in God's welcoming work. No matter who we welcome, God got there first, offering welcome in this person's life long before we showed up. Our inability to see Christ in the stranger doesn't mean Christ isn't there, but that we need to exercise our imaginations!

In chapter 1 we talked about recognition, seeing beyond appearances. This is an act of the imagination, seeing beyond labels or demographic categories, seeing others most deeply for who they are, the gifts and burdens that they bring. If we live in the trust that God has already been at work, we are expectant that, in this visitor, God has something to say to us. If we want to know what Jesus is up to, and the abundant life Jesus has for our church family, we pay attention to this stranger, trusting that in welcoming the stranger, we welcome Christ himself.

Questions to Ponder

+ In whom in your life has it been easy to see Christ? Why?

+ In whom has it been hard to see Christ? Why?

+ How do you know Jesus when you see him?

+ What seeds has God already planted in the strangers you welcome at church?

Experiment

Try the experiment of presuming Jesus is present in each person you encounter. Set aside a day, a half day, or a specific window of time, like a trip to the mall or a meeting at work. Experiment with presuming Jesus is present in each person you encounter. Presume Jesus is present in every cashier or clerk, every person in line, every person around the conference table or on the conference call.

Does this change the way you relate to them? How? Remember, this experiment does not require that you see Jesus in each person, but only that you presume Jesus is there whether you can see it or not. If it helps, begin the experiment with a brief prayer, "Grant me the gift of eyes to see Christ in each person."

Meditation 9:
Releasing Outcomes

Scripture: Matthew 13:3–9

And he told them many things in parables, saying: "Listen! A sower went out to sow. And as he sowed, some seeds fell on the path, and the birds came and ate them up. Other seeds fell on rocky ground, where they did not have much soil, and they sprang up quickly, since they had no depth of soil. But when the sun rose, they were scorched; and since they had no root, they withered away. Other seeds fell among thorns, and the thorns grew up and choked them. Other seeds fell on good soil and brought forth grain, some a hundredfold, some sixty, some thirty. Let anyone with ears listen!" (NRSV)

Reflection

This sower sowed seeds in all kinds of soil, seemingly throwing seeds everywhere. We might think this sower a bit wasteful, sowing seeds even in rocky or thorny soil. The extravagance in this story is striking: the sower plants seeds regardless of the likely outcome. No soil testing is conducted first, no cost analysis of where to invest the seeds to ensure profit. The sower is simply intent upon sowing.

One of the hardest disciplines of a spirituality of hospitality is giving over the outcomes to God. We want to know that we are good stewards of our church's resources, that our investments will produce results. We want to know that our efforts to be hospitable will (literally!) pay off.

Yet our expected outcomes are not always fulfilled. When we don't get the response we expected, we may feel rejected or disappointed. The visitor we greet never returns and we conclude that our welcome failed or was a waste of time. The person we welcomed from rehab relapses back into substance abuse, and we may think our welcome was squandered. Perhaps God feels the same disappointment when God's welcome extended to humanity seems to have little return on God's investment. Still, God's hospitality does not depend on our response. God does not keep score or run a risk analysis before extending hospitality to us. God keeps planting seeds in us, whether our soil is rocky and dry or rich and fertile.

We are sharing God's welcome, and the outcomes belong to God. The real outcomes, the ultimate results, are not necessarily the immediate ones. Sometimes our welcome of others in fact plants seeds in them that will blossom elsewhere at a later time that we may never see. This is hard. Why bother planting seeds when there is no guarantee of what it will produce? I can only imagine the disciples' incredulous response to Jesus' parable of the sower: "Why are we doing all this then?"

Perhaps it's no surprise that Jesus immediately offers another story about seeds, the parable of the mustard seed (Matt. 13:31–32). In this one, a minuscule seed grows into a lush shelter for birds and animals. Staring at a small seed in your hand, it's hard to imagine the mature plant it will become. If you had never seen a watermelon, could you possibly imagine it just from looking at the seed? Laying down our expectations, or at least carrying them lightly in our hands, can be aided by the use of our imaginations. The outcomes of our hospitality may look nothing like the seeds we plant. While our original expectations may not be fulfilled, God is at work creating outcomes we may miss if we're not careful. Which leads us to a caution here: releasing outcomes to God does not mean having low expectations, or guarding against investing ourselves in our efforts toward hospitality. Quite the opposite. We can expect God's welcoming spirit to do amazing work among us. It just means we stay clear that the outcomes belong to God alone.

Questions to Ponder

+ What outcomes do you expect?
+ What if they don't happen?
+ What does success look like?
+ What does failure look like?

Experiment

For an individual: In prayer, think about someone or something you want to welcome. As you lift up this person or area of your life, lay your hands in your lap, palms up. Rest the backs of your hands gently on your legs and feel the air on the surface of the skin on your palms. Feel the emptiness and openness there to receive whatever outcome happens as a gift from God. Open hands represent a hospitable openness to the area or person you are lifting up and a grateful heart, ready to receive whatever outcome emerges. You may find this posture of openness and gratitude aids other prayer as well.

For a group: As your committee develops a hospitality program or plan, focus on one specific effort and brainstorm
specific outcomes. For example, if you have decided to begin
including a time during worship to tell of God's welcome (see
"Telling Times in Worship," page 121 below), brainstorm on
newsprint all the possible outcomes you can imagine from
this new practice. Remember that brainstorming means all
contributions go up on the paper. Get way out there with
the possibilities, outcomes disappointing and heartbreaking
as well as outcomes thrilling and exhilarating. Such a list
might include items like "no one speaks" and "worship runs
too long."

After exhausting all the possibilities, lay that newsprint on
the table and ask the group members to reach their hands onto
the table and place them on the newsprint. With everyone's
hands spread on the paper, say a prayer, laying down your
expectations and all the possible outcomes, giving them over
to God's keeping. Something like:

> We expect great things, Lord, as we live in your welcome
> and offer it to others. We plant the seeds in others that you
> have planted in us.
>
> We give the outcomes into your keeping.
>
> Give us eyes to see the tiniest growth, to smell the faintest
> fragrance, to taste the unexpected fruit.
>
> No matter what, we are blessed to live in your life and we
> give thanks.

Throughout the year, as you implement your plans and seek
to live more deeply in God's welcome, return to this prayer as
a touchstone of your mission.

Meditation 10:
Get Lost! Embrace Disorientation

Scripture: Deuteronomy 10:17–19

For the Lord your God is God of gods and Lord of lords, the great God, mighty and awesome, who is not partial and takes no bribe, who executes justice for the orphan and the widow, and who loves the strangers, providing them food and clothing. You shall also love the stranger, for you were strangers in the land of Egypt. (NRSV)

Reflection

This passage occurs as Israel moves from slavery to freedom. God reminds them of God's own love for strangers, for widows and orphans, that is, for those on the margins. But God takes another step here and ties love for the stranger to Israel's experience of being the stranger. Surely this was an experience that the Israelites wanted to leave behind. We don't want to remember the times we have felt powerless and vulnerable. We want to remember the stories of our victories and accomplishments. God wants them to remember the experience of being the stranger. The message is clear: if we want to love the stranger, it's important to stay in touch with the experience of being the stranger.

The longer we've been in a congregation, the more likely we have lost touch with the disorientation of being a stranger. If we have resided in this congregation for a while, then we know where things are, we know to whom to go, we know how to get things done. We know. To be a stranger is to *not know*. In order to pay attention to God's welcome, we need to keep in touch with that experience of not knowing.

Truth be told, we do have the experiences of being the stranger who doesn't know, but we may not associate it with church. Remember your first day on a new job? You didn't know the code to the copy machine, or what others expected, or who you could trust with questions. Remember moving to a new home? That first trip to the grocery store took twice as long as it would later because you didn't know where everything was. You didn't know who in your new neighborhood would reach out or who would be your children's friends.

The initial period of disorientation in a new job or new home is duplicated in small everyday experiences when we enter the unknown or unfamiliar. Our usual route to work is blocked, and we are rerouted on a detour through unknown streets. Our usual work routine is disrupted by a new computer system that causes disorientation for weeks. Our spouse retires, and our usual home routine is disrupted by unfamiliar patterns as we run into each other all day, and he tries to reorganize the pantry! These experiences of disorientation, of being lost in one's own life, are key experiences of being the stranger who does not know.

We also experience disorientation as a church family: when a pastor leaves and a new pastor arrives; when we realize that the way we've always done things isn't working anymore; when we have genuine disagreement about the ministries of the church. These can be wilderness places where we are lost and do not know our way. This disorientation is a gift that helps us return to being the stranger who does not know.

No doubt being lost or not knowing can be anxiety-producing, so it may be hard to see how it can be part of God's welcome. At the least, it helps us remember the experience of being the stranger. Disorientation gives us compassion and humility for others who are themselves strangers, who don't know our church, our theological views, or our social norms. Being the stranger who does not know keeps that memory fresh and real so that when we welcome strangers into our church family, we are aware of the disorientation and vulnerability that can entail.

The experience of getting lost has within it another gift that is not about how we relate to others, but how we relate to God. Being lost returns us to vulnerability, to powerlessness in a life that is mostly privileged. We are available to God and to God's welcome in a particular way in our lostness. While we may want to quickly relieve the anxiety of unfamiliarity, if we dare stay in that disorientation just a bit, we will find ourselves deeply in God's life. Vulnerability reveals the truth about ourselves — that we cannot do it alone, that we don't know it all, that we are not in control — and so we come to God unmasked. Daily deceptions of privilege make us believe that we can do it alone, that we do know it all, that we are in control. In the face of these deceptions, getting lost is a profound truth-telling, to ourselves and to God. We know God's welcome even when we are lost, even when we are the stranger who does not know. So get lost! And "remember that you were strangers."

Questions to Ponder

* Remember the last time you got lost driving somewhere. What happened? How did you feel?

* How have you experienced God during times of disorientation in your life? Has God seemed absent? Close?

* When you first started attending your current church, in what ways did you feel disoriented — physically, socially, theologically?

Experiment

Get lost. Choose to be a stranger. Visit an unfamiliar church, preferably of a different denomination. If you are mainline Protestant, visit a Roman Catholic, Eastern Orthodox, or Pentecostal congregation for worship. Be present to your own vulnerability, to your uncertainty about where to sit and what to do. Let yourself be a stranger, even if it's uncomfortable. Trust that God will meet you there. Afterward, reflect on what you experienced. What was it like to be a stranger? What hospitality was extended to you? How did you receive it?

Alternative Experiment

Intentionally choose to be a stranger by taking a new route to work or shopping at a different grocery store. This won't be entirely disorientating, but it will give you a taste of disorientation. What do you notice about yourself in the unfamiliar? What frustrations or surprises did you encounter in an unfamiliar situation?

Meditation 11:
Not Enough

Scripture: Matthew 14:15–21

When it was evening, the disciples came to him and said, "This is a deserted place, and the hour is now late; send the crowds away so that they may go into the villages and buy food for themselves." Jesus said to them, "They need not go away; you give them something to eat." They replied, "We have nothing here but five loaves and two fish." And he said, "Bring them here to me." Then he ordered the crowds to sit down on the grass. Taking the five loaves and the two fish, he looked up to heaven, and blessed and broke the loaves, and gave them to the disciples, and the disciples gave them to the crowds. And all ate and were filled; and they took up what was left over of the broken pieces, twelve baskets full. And those who ate were about five thousand men, besides women and children. (NRSV)

Reflection

The anxiety of the disciples is one we know well: we don't have enough to meet the needs before us. We all know the panic of unexpected guests who show up for dinner — will we have enough food to go around? The feeding of the five thousand seems to be a magic trick, but the simple wisdom of the story reminds us to trust that whatever we have is enough. We simply share whatever we have.

Many church families live with a constant chorus of "not enough" — either we are not big enough or financially stable enough or *something* enough. Like the disciples, we look at our paltry resources and despair. The "not enough" mantra can become oppressive and overwhelming: We don't have enough to _____ (fill in the blank here: welcome visitors, help the homeless, feed the hungry, talk to our neighbors, share God's welcome). In a sense, this is true. As the disciples say, "We have nothing here but five loaves and two fish."

But in another sense we have everything we need, because all we ever have to offer is God's welcome. We share that welcome in many forms, but at its base, it is still God's welcome, with or without the bells and whistles. Think about the times you have welcomed people into your home. Some of those times you didn't feel fully prepared, or you wondered if you'd have enough food. You know that these concerns simply go with the territory of hospitality. Our concerns about "not enough" are signs of how deeply we long to be hospitable and how inadequate we feel to this sacred task.

Jesus' feeding in the gospel story radically challenges the cultural messages of "not enough" that bombard us. The view of ourselves that we are not thin enough or smart enough or together enough or whatever-they-are-selling enough seeps into our bones. American culture tends to have a bigger-is-better bias. We have internalized these hypercritical voices and they paralyze us, putting "enough" always just beyond our reach. Tragically, the defeatist refrain that we can never do or be enough undermines God's welcome. The refrain undercuts the simple, sometimes small, usually not glamorous, steps we can take to welcome. Jesus says to the disciples who believe they don't have enough, "Bring to me whatever you have." Jesus meets them where they are, with the little they have, blessing it and using it.

So it is with gospel hospitality. God's welcome tells us we are not primarily consumers who can never have enough or achievers who can never be enough. Instead, God's welcome tells us we are children of God, blessed and welcomed into God's life. Living in God's welcome, we trust the working of the Spirit instead of our own achievement. We let God fill the gaps of our inadequacies. When the fears of "not enough" dominate, return to your experience of God's welcome in your own life as a touchstone. God has already proclaimed that you are enough! God has already received you fully into God's own life. Lean back into God's arms, into God's welcome, and let that be enough.

Questions to Ponder

• Tell about a time in your life when you thought you weren't good enough, or able enough, or prepared enough. What happened?

• What is it you as a congregation think you don't have enough of? What are you waiting for?

• What about hospitality intimidates you or your congregation? Why?

• What would it look like to have enough or be enough?

Experiment

The natural world offers us wonderful reminders to trust that whatever we have is enough. Sit in your yard or park and examine the various plants you encounter — tall, stalky flowers; low, creeping vines; small bushes, tall trees, dry grass. Pick two or three plants to draw. Artistic talent doesn't matter here;

use the eyes of your heart to draw one of the plants on paper. As you draw, meditate upon its origins: a seed or a tuber, flung on the ground by the wind or a bird or a person. A tiny beginning, hardly the flourishing life it appears now. Then draw from your imagination what its origins looked like. This small beginning was enough.

> I am so small!
> How can this great love be inside of me?
> Look at your eyes. They are small.
> But they see enormous things.
>
> — Rumi

Meditation 12:
Welcoming Creation

Scripture: Genesis 1:26–31

God spoke: "Let us make human beings in our image, make them reflecting our nature so they can be responsible for the fish in the sea, the birds in the air, the cattle, and, yes, Earth itself, and every animal that moves on the face of Earth." God created human beings; he created them godlike, reflecting God's nature. He created them male and female. God blessed them: "Prosper! Reproduce! Fill Earth! Take charge! Be responsible for fish in the sea and birds in the air, for every living thing that moves on the face of Earth." Then God said, "I've given you every sort of seed-bearing plant on Earth, and every kind of fruit-bearing tree, given them to you for food. To all animals and all birds, everything that moves and breathes, I give whatever grows out of the ground for food." And there it was. God looked over everything he had made; it was so good, so very good! It was evening, it was morning — Day Six.

(THE MESSAGE)

Reflection

It is rare anymore for many Christians reading Scripture to hear Jesus' parables of seeds and trees with an experiential ear. We don't live close to the earth and its cycles, so the power of those stories is diminished for us. We hear them as quaint stories about gardens and things that grow. How many of us have ever seen a threshing floor or have known the panic of a field that does not yield a harvest? Yet for those whose daily lives depend on retrieving water from the nearest source and eating food cultivated by their own hands, Jesus' images of planting, growing, dying, and rising are very real.

The first account of creation in Genesis describes the glory and beauty of our creating God, a host preparing a home for all sorts of growing things, birds and animals, plants and people. God welcomes all of creation into God's own life. How can we welcome all of creation, too? First, the creation account above suggests that humans, created last, are the hosts, responsible "for every living thing," says God. We are convicted by these words, knowing we have failed to be responsible hosts. Instead we have squandered resources and abused the creation we are charged to welcome.

If we read on into Genesis 2, we discover that we humans are not only the hosts: we are also the guests. God has invited us into this garden of creation, with some warnings about its use. Perhaps we are not the center of the universe as so much of our humanity-centered theology tends to assume. Rather, we are guests, indeed, strangers, who are welcomed by creation. We are dependent upon the natural world for our sustenance and survival. These words convict us, too. We have not been polite or grateful guests, but have taken advantage of our host, hoarding and wasting the resources of the very host world that has welcomed us into its keeping.

The good news is that our faith gives us a new frame of reference for our relationship in and to creation. We are, at the same time, both welcomed guests and responsible hosts. We can receive the natural world as a sacred guest, seeing Christ in this stranger. We can humble ourselves as sojourners who must rely on the generosity of our host for our daily lives. We might call this environmental hospitality, but that almost makes it too separate from the everyday hospitality of our lives. More true to Scripture is the acknowledgement that our participation in God's welcome will include welcoming all creation, oceans and stars, farms and forests.

The implications can be overwhelming. Welcoming creation bears upon everything we do, from the way we mine the planet's natural resources to how we develop chemical fertilizers and genetically enhanced seeds. God's welcome can be proclaimed in our fishing and logging practices and in scales of economy that are sustainable for local ecologies. Right here in our everyday lives, however, most of us are welcoming creation in ways we might not suspect. Gospel hospitality for creation hits very close to home in our daily recycling to reduce landfills, our conservation of water in our homes and lawns, in the cars we drive, and the mass transit we use. These daily practices witness to God's welcome in our lives and to our roles as both responsible hosts and grateful guests. "God looked over everything he had made; it was so good, so very good!"

Questions to Ponder

- Tell about a time you felt welcomed into creation, maybe through a walk in the woods or a flower in your yard that evoked a sense of God's welcome.

- Tell about a time you felt a responsibility to host creation, perhaps by tending your garden or cleaning trash along a waterway.

- In what ways do you think of yourself as a guest on the planet?

- In what ways do you think of yourself as a host who welcomes creation?

- What difference would it make in your life to participate in God's welcome through creation?

Experiment

For an entire day, use no artificial lighting. See if you can go through a day using natural light or candlelight only. (If you spend your day in a work setting with artificial lighting you may have to choose a day you are not at work.) Experience your dependence on the sun and the way it illumines your life. How do you welcome sunlight? How does it welcome you?

Meditation 13:
A Body of Outsiders

Scripture: 1 Corinthians 10:15–17

I speak as to sensible people; judge for yourselves what I say. The cup of blessing that we bless, is it not a sharing in the blood of Christ? The bread that we break, is it not a sharing in the body of Christ? Because there is one bread, we who are many are one body, for we all partake of the one bread. (NRSV)

Reflection

We are all part of the one body. Paul uses this image through-out his letters to remind the early, contentious Christians at Corinth that, no matter how much it seems that some of them are "in" while others are "out," all parts of the body belong to the one body. No part of the body is more in or out than an-other part. Christ's body cannot be chopped up into disparate pieces. We all belong equally because we all share in the table of grace, the cup and the bread.

The struggles of the early Corinthians continue in every generation. We are painfully aware that some Christians claim to be in and declare other Christians are outside the body of Christ. God's welcome is so much bigger than our categories of status.

Many mainline congregations have the reverse problem: a body full of outsiders. Folks who attend, who may have been members for years, continue to see themselves as more out than in. It's hard to be a body with most of the parts disconnected, a congregation made up of observers, members who see themselves on the fringes. This epidemic of outsidership may be especially characteristic of baby boomers, whose identity is rooted in being outsiders who challenge the system, whatever the system is. Outsidership may not be a decision so much as a default for some.

The danger of this self-understanding in our congregational lives is that no one sees themselves as the host, the householder inviting others to the party. Asked whether they routinely seek out and greet visitors to their church, many church folks respond that they don't think it is their job. The greeter or usher does that. The pastor does that. The lay leader does that. That is someone else's responsibility.

Dig deeper and we hear an expression of identity underneath this explanation. The pastor, the lay leader, the church matriarch, the usher, that is, those who have a stake here, or those who have power here, are responsible to offer God's welcome. Though we all share in the one table and the one body, we don't all feel a sense of belonging and insidership. What does hospitality look like when everyone is the guest, the outsider?

Paul's words call us to a new self-understanding. Different parts of the body have genuine differences, yet each part exists only to the degree that it shares in the one body. A disconnected hand or foot has no life. The body of Christ has no lone rangers, no observers. We all share in God's welcome, and God's welcome is the starting place. Each one of us begins with our own experience of God's welcome, whether through disruption or challenge, forgiveness or risk (see chapter 2). Through God's welcome in our lives, we are each members of the body, part of something bigger in which we share and take responsibility to share with others.

Questions to Ponder

+ How would you identify yourself within your congregation — as insider or outsider, as observer or participant?

+ How and why has your self-understanding changed over time?

+ How would you describe your church's membership with regards to outsidership? Do you have a congregation of guests? Why or why not?

+ How do you know whether folks feel inside or outside? How is belonging in your congregation experienced? Demonstrated?

Experiment

Draw a circle that represents your total church membership. Place a dot at the center of the circle. Place an "x" for yourself within that circle. Would you place yourself toward the center or the edges? Outside the circle altogether? Share your circles and x's in pairs. Was it hard to determine where to place your x or did you know right away? Do you wish your x were in a different place? What do you long for?

Alternative Experiment

Think about your church as a body. What part of the body are you? Which part of the human body best reflects your sense of your own part in your congregation? Maybe you're an eye that brings vision or an ear that listens. In pairs, share the body part you identify with and why. Was it hard to determine a body part or did you know right away? Do you wish you were a different part? What do you long for?

Meditation 14:
They Will Know Us by Our Love

Scripture: John 13:34–35

I give you a new commandment, that you love one another. Just as I have loved you, you also should love one another. By this everyone will know that you are my disciples, if you have love for one another. (NRSV)

Reflection

Jesus tells his followers that love is the primary characteristic by which they will be known. Wow! Imagine if Christians in America were known by our love. Imagine that people you encounter every day expected you to be a loving person con-cerned with the welfare of others because you are a follower of Jesus. Sadly, in the current cultural climate, many people would assume just the opposite — that Christians are people primarily interested in judging others.

Popular culture is full of these images: Dana Carvey made a career of his caricature, "the church lady," on *Saturday Night Live.* The church lady was always ready with a quick judgment, a sarcastic question, or a suspicious sneer. Carvey could masterfully conjure the nasal twang, "Maybe it's *Satan?*"

TV evangelists are another favorite caricature in the popular media, the Bible-thumping, money-begging, slick-haired preacher who is crying doom if you don't call the number on your TV screen right now with a financial gift. The movie *Saved* shows the stereotypical Christian displaying hostility for another person through a veneer of love. As Hilary, the main character, walks away in disgust at another teenager who refuses to do her bidding, she slams her Bible against the car door, shouting, "I love Jesus!" In general, American popular culture has sent the message loud and clear: Christians are judgmental, self-righteous, and bullying.

At the heart of these portrayals is the notion that Christians are concerned first and foremost with keeping score for reward and punishment — deciding who's going to heaven and who's going to hell. In fact, many Christians themselves believe that's what they should be concerned about. The idea that Christianity is about scorekeeping, heaven and hell, distorts the gospel with fear: Will I be good enough? Will I get a ticket into heaven? This is a far cry from the good news of God's welcome: "God's welcome is at hand!" (Mark 1:15; Luke 4:43). Fear-mongering among Christians violates rather than fosters the good news of God's welcome. The scorekeeping version of Christianity is neither biblical nor faithful and leaves people frightened and alienated.

In contrast to portrayals of Christians, depictions of Jesus in popular culture are more inviting. Jesus may suffer (*The Passion of Christ*), or be misunderstood (*The Life of Brian*), but he is rarely hostile to others in film or TV. In general, the popular view is that Jesus is interested in love, mercy, and healing. A big disconnect between popular views of Christians and popular views of Christ. Jesus offers welcome, but Christians don't.

We repair this disconnect by returning to the new commandment, to love one another so that all will know Jesus'

followers by our love. Paying attention to God's welcome concretely in our everyday lives directs us back to love. Each new
day brings another chance to live the new commandment of
love. Jesus' words — to be known by our love — were given to
the disciples just before Jesus' crucifixion, parting instructions
for their journey ahead and for ours, too. These words, to live
and proclaim love, embolden us in the face of distortions that
present Christianity as an unwelcoming faith.

When the rest of us remain silent in the face of the dis-
torted gospel of scorekeeping presented by some Christian
brothers and sisters, we endorse the lie. Like children on
a playground afraid to challenge the bully, our passivity allows Christians to hurt others and damages the gospel of
Jesus Christ. We don't have to attack other Christians or
judge them. We simply have to speak the truth we know, the
welcome we have received, free of charge, into abundant life.

Questions to Ponder

+ What popular portrayals of Christians come to mind?

+ What portrayals of Christians do you resonate with or
  reject? Why?

+ What portrayal of Christians would you like to see? Why?

+ How do you respond to Christians focused on scorekeeping? How would you like to respond?

Experiment

Most congregations are full of folks who have been trauma-
tized by Christians who, however well-meaning, bullied them
with "If you died tonight, do you know where you'd go?" or
with an unrelenting sense of God's anger and disappointment
in them, much like the God of Stan's childhood (see page 27
above). Invite some of those folks to share their stories. This is
painful for us to hear, to face the damage Christian churches

have done by creating fear, especially among children. But it's important to give voice to these hurtful chapters because this testimony prods us to not remain silent, to bear witness to God's welcome. Ask these same folks to tell what they wish other Christians had said or done in the face of this fear-mongering. Listen to their longings for us to be known by our love.

Alternative Experiment

Next time you hear another Christian bullying others with a gospel of scorekeeping, or frightening others with threats of hell, experiment by sharing your own experience of God's good news. We don't have to attack other Christians or judge them. We simply have to speak the truth we know, the welcome we have received into abundant life. Think about what you would say. Something like: "All I can say is, that's not the God I know. In my life, Jesus has brought challenge, for sure, but God has opened my eyes to all the grace around me." Or, "Wow, really? The God I know brings blessings into my life everyday — my wife, my kids. And God didn't make me pass a test first. They are sheer gifts." What would you say?

Chapter 4

The Feast
of Salvation

We've looked at all the ways God welcomes us into abundant life, into "a wide-open, spacious life" (2 Cor. 6:11, THE MESSAGE). We've explored God's welcome in Scripture, and in our daily lives. In the last chapter, we experimented with practices that pay attention to God's welcome. As Christians, we have a theological word for this ongoing welcome of God: "salvation." Salvation is the *continual presence and activity of God in our lives,* welcoming us deeper into the divine life through being a disciple of Jesus Christ.

Salvation: God's Welcome in Every Moment and Molecule

For many Christians, salvation means going to heaven when we die, but the Bible promises much more. Salvation is present and ongoing, not just a future reward. Salvation is here, now, as we live every day in God's life. Salvation is God's salve-ing, putting medicine, the salve of grace on the whole breadth, length, height, and depth of our lives. God is constantly renewing us, saving/salving us, welcoming us to abundant life. While we often picture God in the clouds somewhere, our faith claims we have a God living right here who fills every nook and cranny of life. God's salving/saving welcome spans from the earliest love planted in our lives, across our whole lives, all the way to ultimate union with God after death.[1]

"Salvation" sounds like a heavy church-speak word. It's fallen out of use in many Christian circles, partly because of the way some Christians have used the word hurtfully, and partly because we have let the word "salvation" become puny, small, irrelevant. We can reclaim an expansive view of salvation, in its richness and blessing, but it has traction only when we use it in the landscape of our concrete, messy lives. What does real life, in all its fragmentation, have to do with God's welcome? What does God's welcome have to do with where life really happens? What of that moment, sitting in traffic, staring at the red light? What about that late night conversation with my spouse, the only exchange of sentences for the day, unsatisfying and incomplete? What about IM-ing with friends, or surfing the Web? What of that first morning taste of coffee when the day stands before me, open and possible? We may have a vague sense that God is somehow present in those moments, but we are unlikely to call them salvation. We might not suspect these moments have anything to do with our salvation, or that God is really at work welcoming us into God's abundant life in those moments.

Everything we do, every conversation we have, every task we pursue, every meal we cook, God's saving work is in it all. God's salving/saving fills our congregational lives, too: in Sunday worship and youth lock-ins, in committee meetings and mission trips, in mowing the lawn and tending the nursery. But it doesn't stop there. God's expansive, welcoming work is going on outside our own congregations as well. God's saving work — salvation — is bigger than us, bigger than our church,

---

1. John Wesley's well-known description of God's saving work is "the entire work of God." I owe my description to his discussion in "Scripture Way of Salvation." See *John Wesley,* ed. Albert C. Outler (New York: Oxford University Press, 1964), 271ff.

bigger even than our denomination. Salvation cannot be contained. This is especially good news when we despair of the foibles of our all-too-human congregations.

The whole of each of our lives and our life together is the landscape for God's welcoming, salving work. Salvation is happening all the time. God's welcome is happening all the time. It is a welcome feast.

This is good news indeed, and one that people are hungry to hear. This good news is so deep in the bones of the Christian message that we may take it for granted. When we take it for granted, however, we withhold the food of grace from those who are spiritually hungry. Too many people have heard that salvation is something God will grant once they get their act together, or once they start going to church or reading the Bible. For others, salvation is a ticket they got one time on their knees and now they must wait for the real thing after they die.

The good news we have to share of God's welcome promises much more. God's welcome happens whether we are faithful or not. God's welcome happens whether we respond or not. God's welcome comes from unexpected people and places in our lives. God's welcome comes even amid scarcity, and it is persistent. The good news of salvation is that God's welcome happens in a nanosecond and over a lifetime. God's welcome is working at the molecular and at the cosmic level. I would put it this way: in every moment and in every molecule, God is welcoming us deeper into the divine life. Powerful good news!

Salvation Belongs to God

When we proclaim salvation in gospel hospitality we are not giving people something they don't have. We have no property rights to the welcome table; it belongs to God. We are only pointing out God's saving welcome, paying attention to it, and giving glory to God for it. Since God is already at work in all things, God has already been at work in the experiences people bring with them, even if deeply buried. Whether a visitor or a longtime church member, folks bring experiences from work or school, where God teaches lessons about ourselves, our abilities, and our dreams. People bring experiences from personal relationships, where God is revealing just how deep love goes, or inviting us to offer forgiveness to another, where we stand amazed to see how God has already been there planting seeds. We already know about salvation from our experiences of the natural world, its fierce beauty and insistent cycles of death and rebirth. Yet these experiences of God's welcome may be unnamed, buried in our awareness. Once we name and connect the dots of these experiences, we can see God's saving work in our lives. Gospel hospitality invites people to the welcome feast where we connect the dots of all those experiences. At the welcome table we help each other see God's welcome in our own lives.

Connecting the dots and claiming God's work in our lives is a powerful experience that fills us to spilling over. Like a cup overflowing, God's saving welcome cannot be contained within our lives, and so we extend it to others. We welcome others to the table, not because we want more people on the church rolls, but because we know the deep joy and challenge of sharing life in God, and long for all of creation to share in it, too. Gospel hospitality shifts our attention away from what we have to offer and toward what God has to offer, an expansive table where all can feed on an abundance of mercy and grace.

Our daily Christian walk is nothing more or less than paying attention to the good news of God's welcome in our lives and in the world. We cannot keep this light under a bushel (Matt. 5:15). In the face of the world's constant messages of exclusion, division, resignation, and unwelcome, we proclaim the good news, inviting others to the welcome feast, testifying to the good news of God's welcome to all, which we each already know and already have.

The Pattern of God's Welcome: Jesus

Often the language of salvation in Christian life centers on Jesus, and rightly so. Jesus Christ is the primary pattern of God's welcome. Through God's Incarnation in Jesus Christ, God's welcome is made plain as the welcome of human life itself into the divine life. Our expansive view of salvation comes from the church's historic teaching on the Incarnation.

Put most simply, the doctrine[2] of the Incarnation teaches that God became flesh and dwelt among us (John 1:14). The verb used in John for "dwelt" is the word for pitching a tent or making a home.[3] In this wording, God became flesh and pitched God's tent among us. The doctrine of the Incarnation teaches that God doesn't just drop in for a visit or try on human nature like a pair of pants, but rather, that God makes a home in human being itself. This is a God who lives, day in and day out, not on a cloud far off or some otherworldly realm, but right here, among us, one of us.

Further, the doctrine of the Incarnation teaches that God became flesh and dwelt among us in the person of Jesus Christ. God took on the fullness of human being — all of it — in the person of Jesus Christ. The word itself, "incarnation," incorporates the word *carne*, which means meat or flesh. Incarnation conveys a bloody, concrete, physical expression.

---

2. The word "doctrine" means "teaching."

3. Greek *skenoō*, "to pitch or inhabit a tent." See *Theological Dictionary of the New Testament*, ed. Gerhard Kittel, Geoffrey W. Bromiley, and Gerhard Friedrich (Grand Rapids: Wm. B. Eerdmans, 1985), 1:1043.

God is en-fleshed, given meat. Jesus Christ is the enfleshment of God.

When Christians try to talk about the enfleshment of God, we usually tell the Christmas story of Jesus in the manger. This story is deceptively simple, and often told without an attending awareness of just how troublesome the enfleshment of God is. It may seem unproblematic to us because we have received the Incarnation of God in Jesus as a fully developed teaching. For the earliest Christians, however, the claim that God became flesh and dwelt among us, and more specifically, that God was born of a woman, suffered, and died, was an enormous puzzle. It did not make sense on the most basic levels and it threatened to bring scorn on this fledgling faith.

Yet finally, it is precisely this claim — that *in Jesus Christ God called, fully embraced, and welcomed human nature itself into God's own life* — that is the ground of salvation.

God's Welcome Doesn't Make Sense

In the early Christian world, the claim of the Incarnation was troublesome for several reasons. First, Christian teaching about the Incarnation is a category confusion of the first order. In the ancient world, gods are part of the supernatural world and humans are part of the natural world. Deities and humans may indeed have encounters and deities can move easily within both natural and supernatural realms. A god is never confused with a human being, however, and a god never subjects himself or herself to the limits of the natural order. That is, a god would never be subject to the finitude that human beings experience, especially birth, illness, suffering, and death. By definition, deities transcend these experiences. While a god might morph into human or animal form for a day, such a god would not submit to the humiliations of finitude like birth or suffering.

In this case, the humiliations God suffered were severe. Jesus had been born in a manger, a powerless baby, a nobody. Hardly a noble start. Further, Jesus had been subjected to a painful death on the cross. What sort of god put up with that? The whole point of being divine is to conquer your enemies, not fall prey to their designs. Worst of all, Jesus Christ actually died, a logical impossibility for a deity. How is it possible for the God who created heaven and earth to die? Was the cosmos without a god until the resurrection? How is this possible? God's welcome in Jesus doesn't make sense.

Second, the teaching of the Incarnation raises the question: What sort of god is interested in this category confusion? Any deity worth his or her salt is a god of power and might. A god has everything to lose and nothing to gain by crossing over from divine into human. This shows extremely poor judgment on the god's part. Certainly it is reasonable to ask whether such a god who is willing to lose status by taking on the form and limits of humanity is even trustworthy. A self-demoting god does not inspire trust or confidence among humans desperately needing to be delivered from the very humanity the god has assumed. God's welcome in Jesus doesn't make sense.

Third, in order to make sense of this central claim that God became flesh in Jesus Christ, early Christians came up with several explanations that soften the sharp edges of this outrageous claim. At the heart of these various explanations is the notion that God didn't really become 100 percent human. To counter the ridiculous idea that the God of the universe would submit to being born and limited by a human body, it made more sense to argue that Jesus only appeared to be human. In this view, Jesus' physical body was a phantom, appearing human to those around him, while in truth just a pretend body. According to this explanation, God never really suffered the humiliation of birth, pain on the cross, or actual death. Instead, God fooled us with a fake body and preserved the integrity of divinity all along.

Similarly, some Christians could not stomach the idea of God growing inside a woman's womb and, even worse, God going through the contamination of the bloody mess of a woman's birth canal. To claim that God was born in this way was going too far, argued these Christians, and dishonored God. Instead, they suggested it makes more sense for God to have entered the human Jesus at some later point, perhaps when he was reading in the temple at age twelve. Surely that is a more appropriate time for the divine to possess a human body, filling Jesus with divine spirit. According to this explanation, God stays fully spirit and adopts a human body, which can be discarded at a later date. The whole idea of a God-human being does challenge all our categories and worldviews. Most of the theological controversies of the first five hundred years of Christianity address the problem of the Incarnation in one way or another.

It's no surprise that these struggles haven't gone away. God's welcome in Jesus still doesn't make sense. Christians today struggle too with how to think about Jesus Christ as God incarnate. Is Jesus 50/50 human/divine? 40/60? Maybe 30/70? Can we divide the scriptural accounts of his life with some words of Scripture referring to his humanity and some referring to his divinity? Perhaps his wonder-working was his divine nature and his anger in the temple was his human nature? Our questions try to make sense of it

"God became flesh and dwelt among us," 100 percent God and 100 percent human. God welcomed human life by becoming fully human. Many of us still think of Jesus' humanity as fundamentally different from our own. It is hard for us to imagine that in Jesus Christ God has welcomed all the human experiences we find broken or shameful. Did Jesus experience human being the way I experience it, that is, with petty feelings, even sin? Christians today may be more subtle, but we are not far from the heresies of the first three centuries. Indeed, it stretches our normal reasoning to claim that God became flesh and dwelt among us in the person of Jesus Christ, born, suffered, died, was buried, and rose from the dead.

Divine Hospitality: God's Welcome to Humanity

If the doctrine of the Incarnation was such a problem for early Christians, why did they cling to it and why should we? Why not discard this pesky teaching for a more plausible one? At stake in the doctrine of the Incarnation is salvation itself. In the Incarnation God did more than dress up as a human being. In the Incarnation, God welcomed human being, all of human nature, into the divine life, to heal and restore it. To save it.

In this welcome, God is host and humanity is the stranger welcomed in. Through the Incarnation, God has welcomed the stranger, human nature, invited it home, and restored it. As with any act of welcome, the host and guest do not remain unchanged, but are transformed by hospitality. God genuinely experiences human finitude, and human being genuinely experiences divine healing. The teaching of the Incarnation that God took all of human being into the divine life for a dwelling place means every part of human life dwells in God.

The parts of the gospel story that offended ancient hearers, namely, God submitting to the indignities of human existence, are the parts of the gospel story that proclaim salvation. Perhaps most powerful in the Incarnation in Jesus is God's voluntary vulnerability to human hate and violence, culminating in the crucifixion. Jesus' life, ministry, and crucifixion show us that hospitality requires risk, calls for living in hard places, and doesn't always look like success by the world's standards.

God's welcome of human being into God's own life is not a partial welcome. In Jesus Christ, God did not offer the divine life to us as a vacation spot, a place where we reside only if we're good, or only if we're healthy, or only if we deny the flawed finitude that makes us human. No. God did not pick and choose which part of human life to embrace. The gospel story tells us that God in Jesus Christ embraced it all: along with friendship and joy, Jesus experiences frustration, temp-tation, betrayal, suffering, and even death. God welcomes it all — birth, suffering, death, along with joy, confusion, and love, all the dimensions of being human. Only by fully em-bracing all the dimensions of human being can God offer full salvation. If God did not fully welcome human frailty and sin into the divine life, then human frailty and sin could not be healed. If God did not welcome suffering and death into the divine life through the suffering and death of Jesus Christ, then suffering and death could not be conquered. God's wel-come of human nature, in all its messiness and indignity, through the Incarnation in Jesus Christ, salves/saves us.

God's welcome for each of us is what is at stake in the doctrine of the Incarnation. Because God became flesh and dwelt among us, pitched God's tent with us in Jesus Christ, we are welcomed into the dwelling place of God's own life, where we can be redeemed and healed. Salvation is nothing more or less than being welcomed into God's life, where we live in the realm of grace.

At Home in God

If God welcomes us into God's own life, then that's where we live; that's our home. It's striking how often the words "home," "dwelling place," "abide," and "belong" are used in

Scripture to talk about our life in God. (Check out Exod. 29:45–46, 2 Sam. 7:4–17, Ps. 23, Jer. 7:3–7, John 1:14, Eph. 3:16–17, 1 John 4:11–13). Can you imagine God as home? God's welcome opens up God's life as home for us to live abundantly. We think of home as the place we belong. We belong to the people there and to the place itself. Home is the center out of which we live. Think of the places in your life you feel most at home, the people with whom you feel at home. These are the places of deep rest and joy, the places you go to find yourself when you are lost and to gain strength in the midst of life's struggles.

Paul's letter to the Romans describes this home-making as God taking up residence in our lives, so that we may dwell in God. Paul puts it this way, "for you who welcome him, in whom he dwells — even though you still experience all the limitations of sin — you yourself experience life on God's terms. It stands to reason, doesn't it, that if the alive-and-present God who raised Jesus from the dead moves into your life, he'll do the same thing in you that he did in Jesus, bringing you alive to himself? When God lives and breathes in you (and he does, as surely as he did in Jesus), you are delivered from that dead life. With his Spirit living in you, your body will be as alive as Christ's! . . . God's Spirit beckons. There are things to do and places to go!" (Rom. 8:10–14, THE MESSAGE). God makes a home in us and we make a home in God.

Home tells us who we are. Home shapes and forms us. As Kathy (see page 42 above) was welcomed into God's life through recovery, more and more she made her home there. She found that her identity was less and less dependent on the expectations of those around her and her self-medicating. Instead her identity was grounded in God's welcome, seeing herself as a child of God, knowing love at the center of things. At home in God, Kathy was more able to offer welcome to others. For Tom (see page 40 above), making a home in God's

welcome meant he saw his own worth less and less tied to
employment status or income. Instead, he experienced more
and more his own sacred worth and in turn, the sacred worth
of others. At home in God, in "an open, spacious life," we
discover our truest identity.

We celebrate this home-making in God each time we take
communion. Jesus says, "Those who eat my flesh and drink
my blood abide in me and I in them" (John 6:56 NRSV). We
abide, we make a home, in Christ, just as God made a home
in humanity. We remember and reclaim that home in communion. "Abide in me as I abide in you...abide in my love"
(John 15:4, 9 NRSV). All who hunger for mercy, for the welcome that heals and saves, come to this welcome feast to be
fed, to find a home. The communion table represents God's
welcome, our home.

Evangelism at Its Best: Living the Good News of God's Welcome

As we celebrate God's welcome in our lives, we are doing
evangelism at its best. "Evangelism" comes from the root
word *evangel*, which means good news. Unfortunately, the
church today is pretty confused about what evangelism is.
Some think evangelism is persuading others to believe cer-
tain ideas. Others think evangelism is getting people to join
the church.

At its best, evangelism is living out and sharing the good
news of God's welcome so naturally and deeply that others
claim the good news of God's welcome in their own lives, too.
The good news is real and compelling when it comes from the
truth of our lives, not when it is a set of right words. When
evangelism focuses on ideas only, on telling others what they
should think, it lacks biblical credibility, because that's not

the way Jesus did it. Jesus gives us the model for evangelism in the Gospels — he *lives* the good news. Jesus doesn't just talk the talk. He walks the walk. Jesus' ministry rarely focuses on telling people what to believe or think.[4] Jesus offers people the *experience* of God's welcome, concrete and real. He says, "God's welcome [kingdom of God] is right here, right now, and you can start on a new path [repent]" (Matt. 4:17, Mark 1:15, author's translation). Jesus calls people to turn. He offers the concrete experience of that welcome in healing, feasting, fellowshipping, and praying.

That's why we are careful to avoid telling others *about* God's welcome. Gospel hospitality is not telling others *about* God, but sharing our experience *of* God. Gospel hospitality is a lived reality, a way of being in the world.

I want to be careful here not to fall into the false dichotomy between words and actions in evangelism, as though we need only do one or the other. Evangelism is both/and, of course: we share the experience of God's welcome through both words and actions. Words without the testimony of our lives are hollow. On the other hand, actions without words may not be enough for folks who are lonely, lost, burdened, or unwelcome in their everyday lives. They are hungry to be welcomed from death to life, from shame to forgiveness, from wandering in an alien land to coming home. Justice demands that we use words to make plain God's welcome to all kinds of strangers.

Evangelism, then, is *offering the experience of God's welcome through words and actions.* Our experience of being welcomed by God into abundant life is something we are compelled to share, like the birth of a baby or the homecoming of a lost

---

4. Jesus does say, in English translation, "*believe* the good news" (Mark 1:15). Our modern ears are likely to hear "believe" as a propositional statement requiring cognitive assent akin to believing that $2+2=4$ or that the sky is blue. Jesus is offering something different here: "believe" is a new orientation of the heart in trust, more akin to believing in someone you love or trusting in the future. Believing the good news is a way of life, not an ideological platform.

son. It seeps from our pores and pervades all we say and do. Sharing God's welcome with others is organic to our lives. Evangelism calls us to be thoughtful, careful, and intentional in offering the experience of God's welcome so that others can participate more deeply, too. We do this when we say, "Look! See! God's welcome is near."

Evangelism is not only a proclamation of good news to those outside the church. Those in the church are hungry for it, too. We count on each other to claim God's welcome when we have become too busy to pay attention, or when our lives have become too painful to know God's welcome is near. When I lost my daughter, brave Christians walked with me through that dark time, never pushing, but always pointing to God's offer of abundant life, of welcome. Their lives and their love showed me that my grief was not the end of the story. They were evangelists, sharing the good news with me so genuinely that my life was renewed, and I walked more deeply with God after that.

Evangelism need not be scary. While some may shout from street corners or knock on doors, that is not the only, or even the best, way to share the good news. Evangelism needs to always point to the experience of God's welcome, not to ourselves, not to our church, not to a set of ideas. The good news can be known only in the reality of the living God, breathing through our lives, offering continual welcome. Your very life bears the good news. You are an evangelist. A life of intentional seeking and sharing God's welcome, a life of risking and repentance, a life in committed community, testifying to the amazing welcome of God's life shouts the good news as concrete, real, and compelling truth. Gospel hospitality — seeing God's welcome, living God's welcome, and extending that welcome to others — is a life of evangelism. You are enough. Trust your welcome into God's life. You know it as truly as it can be known.

We all feed at God's welcome feast in every moment and molecule of our lives. We invite others to share in the feast, but the table belongs to God. It takes practice, helping each other see and celebrate God's welcome in the mundane and the extraordinary.

Benediction

God has welcomed each of us.
We live in the abundant life of God's welcome.
You don't need to become someone or something else.
Just live in the welcome you already know.
You have it.
Now claim it, share it, and give thanks to God.

Study Group Exercises

These seed-planting exercises can be used with a hospitality study group, with a hospitality planning group, in a retreat setting, or for individual reflection. Select the exercises for each chapter that best suit your group, and adapt them as needed. Don't try to use them all. You may need to prepare the soil of your group by establishing a sense of trust and allowing plenty of time for each exercise so that the seeds can take root. As seeds, these exercises are starting places that require cultivation and patience in order to grow and bear fruit. These exercises work best in groups of no more than six.

Chapter 1 / Gospel Hospitality

1. Getting Started

Share stories of welcome, when you have either received or offered welcome. Springboard questions include:

- Tell about a time you were welcomed when you were a stranger.

- What about this experience made you feel welcome? Do you recall particular words, attitudes, or behaviors?

- Tell about a time you welcomed a stranger. What did you do? How was it received?

- How have your experiences of welcome changed your views of yourself, of others, of God, of world?

- Have your experiences of welcome ever been risky?

+ Have you ever been recognized for more than you appeared to be?

+ Did other stories come to mind as you read the chapter?

What insights about the experience of welcome have emerged from this discussion? What lessons do you carry from these experiences?

2. Bible Study

Explore the story of Genesis 18:1–15. Read it aloud and describe the welcome Abraham and Sarah offer.

+ What in the story is important to you?

+ What would you have done if you were Abraham? Sarah? The strangers?

+ In what ways do you see God's welcome in the story?

3. Congregational Life

What is at stake for this congregation in offering hospitality? Why are you interested?

4. Writing a Litany

This chapter discusses the spiritual marks, or orientations of the heart, that mark the path of hospitality. When you reflect on your experiences of being welcomed and of welcoming others, how have the spiritual marks of readiness, risk, repentance, and recognition accompanied these experiences? Review the current life of your congregation. Where do you see readiness, risk, repentance, and recognition already demonstrated? With your pastor or worship leader, write a litany of thanksgiving for these experiences of gospel hospitality.

5. Monday Morning Connections

Where at school or work do you see the spiritual marks of readiness, risk, repentance, and recognition emerge? What does hospitality look like at work? At school? In your extended family? In your community?

Chapter 2 / God's Welcome

1. Getting Started

Discuss as a group the idea of God's welcome using the questions below to guide your discussion.

- Which of the stories in the chapter resonate with your experience of God's welcome?

- What other ways have you experienced God's welcome or seen it in others?

2. God's Welcome in Our Lives

Select three or four questions from the list below that are most helpful for your group discussion. Take time to hear the stories people have to tell and to explore the similarities and differences in responses within the group.

- Tell about a time in your life when you experienced God's welcome in some way.

- What changed in your life as a result of God's welcome? How did you see yourself differently? God differently? Others differently? Your church family differently?

- Was it easier to experience God's welcome when you were a child or as an adult? Why?

- What role have others played in your experience of God's welcome?

- What role has the church played in your experience of God's welcome?

- When you have experienced God's welcome, did you receive it or reject it, and in either case, how?

- Tell about a time in your life when you felt like a stranger to God.

- Tell about a time in your life when you experienced God as a stranger in your life.

- How have these experiences changed over your life stages and circumstances?

- How has your church family experienced God's welcome?

- When has your church family felt like a stranger to God?

Listen for insights about experiencing God's welcome. What do you hear?

3. Bible Study

Offer a four-to-six-week Bible study on God's welcome in Scripture. Each week, explore one Bible story, looking for God's welcome. Choose from the list below or use the week's lectionary texts.

- Creation: Genesis 1–2:3 and 2:4–3

- Abraham and Sarah under the oaks of Mamre: Genesis 18:1–15

- Moses story: Exodus 2

- Israelites in the wilderness: Exodus 15:22–16

- Rahab helps Joshua's spies: Joshua 2 and 6

- Ruth and Naomi: Ruth

- Widow of Zarephath: 1 Kings 17:8–16

- Incarnation in Jesus Christ: John 1:1–16

- Household has a banquet: Matthew 22:1–14, Luke 14:16–24;

- Parable of the lost sons: Luke 15:11–32

- Woman at the well: John 4:4–42

- Zacchaeus and Jesus: Luke 19:1–10

- Feeding the five thousand: Matthew 14:13–21, Mark 6:30–44, Luke 9:10–17, John 6:1–14

In addition to the questions your own interests prompt, ask:

- Who offers hospitality in the story?
- What does hospitality look like?
- What sort of welcome, if any, does God offer?
- How would you describe God's M.O. in the story?

4. Tag Team Talkback

Select a Bible story above and role play a conversation between God and a character in the passage. One person will speak as a character in the story, for example, Sarah, while another person will speak as God. What would God and the person in the story have to say to each other about welcome? There are no right or wrong answers, just an improvised conversation.

After the first couple of minutes, allow other group members to tag in, tapping one role player to take a place and pick up the conversation. Conversely, either role player can tag out by tapping another person in the group to take their place and pick up the role play. The tag team approach often serves to make the role play lower risk, as role players know they can tag out whenever they want. It also allows the group to explore, through various group members, a variety of perspectives for God and for the character in the story. This exercise requires a basic trust level in a group, and is often a lot of fun.

5. Telling Times

Incorporate a short time of telling about God's welcome in your lives at the beginning of church council meetings. Plan to spend five to ten minutes responding to the questions, "Where has God's welcome been present in your life over the last week?" and "Where have you seen God's welcome in our church family over the last month?" There are no right or wrong answers. The "telling time" is simply to practice paying attention to God's welcome. The first few times may be mostly full of silence. That's fine. Let people ponder. It's also okay to invite one or two people to think about this ahead of time and break the ice. These "telling times" can be incorporated into any church committee, working group, or class.

6. Telling Times in Worship

You can also incorporate a short "telling time" during worship. Invite congregants to reflect silently or respond orally to the questions, "Where has God's welcome been present in your life over the last week?" and "Where have you seen God's welcome in our church family?" Again, if you invite people to share out loud, the first couple of times may be mostly full of silence. That's fine. Let people ponder. It's also okay to recruit one or two people to think about this ahead of time and break the ice.[1]

7. Writing a Liturgy

With the pastor or worship leader, write a liturgy that lifts up your church's experience of God's welcome throughout the life of the church. Consider using this liturgy regularly during services in which communion is celebrated. The Communion Table itself is a concrete experience of God's invitation to abundant life.

8. The Land of Welcome

Invite the children in your church (or a Sunday school class) to draw a mural entitled, "The Land of Welcome." Using a

---

1. For an inviting discussion of telling our stories, see Lillian Daniel, "Grace Breaking In," in *From Nomads to Pilgrims: Stories from Practicing Congregations*, ed. Diana Butler Bass and Joseph Stewart-Sicking (Herndon, VA: Alban Institute, 2006), and *Tell It Like It Is: Reclaiming the Practice of Testimony* (Herndon, VA: Alban Institute, 2005).

six-to-ten-foot length of butcher paper, children can draw pictures of a landscape (trees, lakes, grass, mountains, etc.) and the ways they experience God's welcoming love — through their families, through nature, through friends, through Scripture — each in their own way. Their drawings will describe the landscape of God's welcome. Hang the mural in the entrance hallway of your church or on a sanctuary wall as a signpost to pay attention to God's welcome.

9. Welcome on the Web

For churches that are electronically literate, use the church website to highlight stories of God's welcome of all people into abundant life. Identify stories in the secular or religious press that point to God's welcome and provide online links to those stories. Also consider devoting a page on your website to your own congregation's stories of God's welcome. You can post a record of stories shared in the "telling times," removing individuals' names for anonymity as necessary.

10. Keep a Welcome Journal

For an individual: Like the popular "gratitude journals" that help folks pay attention each day to the things they are grateful for, a welcome journal can help us pay attention as individuals to God's welcome in our lives. Each day, write down one way you have seen God's welcome, either in your life, someone else's life, your church's life, the larger society, or the natural world. Just a few sentences a day will habituate your eyes to see God's welcome.

For a group: You can adapt the welcome journal to a group such as a Bible study or committee. Post newsprint on the wall and invite people to jot down a note about their experience of God's welcome that week as they enter class or, at the end of the class, about their experience of God's welcome during the group's time together. Over time, each sheet of newsprint adds a page to your group's welcome journal.

11. Monday Morning Connections

How does God welcome you through your weekly activities at home, school, or work?

Chapter 3 / Practicing Gospel Hospitality

The meditations of chapter 3 can be used to plant seeds in group or individual study. Here are some possible formats:

1. Select one or two meditations as weekly options for a study group reading through the book.

2. Select one or two meditations as weekly options to accompany the six-week Bible study suggested in study group exercises for chapter 2 on page 119.

3. Chapter 3 can stand alone as a ten-week hospitality exploration. Each week use one meditation, read the Scripture passage and reflection together, and discuss the questions to ponder. Introduce the experiment and discuss its implementation that week for each person. Upon gathering the following week, begin with sharing experiences of the experiment before turning to the next meditation.

4. Use one meditation as a devotion to open church council or other committee meetings. Use the Scripture passage, reflection, and one discussion question for a brief devotion.

5. For a year, include one meditation in your church newsletter each month to encourage individual exploration of God's welcome.

6. For a year, post one meditation each month on your church website to encourage individual exploration of God's welcome.

Chapter 4 / The Feast of Salvation

1. Getting Started

Select three or four questions from the list below that are most helpful for your group discussion. Take time to hear the stories people have to tell and to explore the similarities and differences in responses within the group.

How have you experienced welcome from others?

- Tell about a time you were welcomed when you were a stranger.
- What about this experience was welcoming? Do you recall particular words, attitudes, or behaviors?
- Tell about a time you were welcomed within your own family, perhaps after a long absence or change in life circumstance.
- How have your experiences of welcome changed you?
- How have your experiences of welcome changed your views of yourself, of others, of God, of the world?
- Imagine yourself being welcomed into a specific new situation that is coming up in your life. What do you hope will happen?
- Have you been welcomed in your church family? In what ways?
- Tell about a time you did not feel welcomed.
- What about this experience was not welcoming? Do you recall particular words, attitudes, or behaviors?
- What are the points of similarity and difference in your and others, answers to these questions?

Next, select three or four questions from the list below. Again, take time to hear stories and explore the range of experiences.

How have you welcomed others?

+ Tell about a time you welcomed a stranger. What did you do? How did the stranger respond?

+ When you expect guests at your home, what do you do to prepare? Get specific: Do you send them directions? Do you plan a menu? Clean house?

+ When expected guests arrive, how do you welcome them? Do you greet guests at the door? What happens next? Do you take their coats? Make introductions?

+ When unexpected guests come to your home, how do you welcome them?

+ Have you ever been aware of extending God's welcome to others? Tell about it.

+ Is there a difference in your mind between offering your own welcome and offering God's welcome? If so, what is it? If not, why not?

+ How has welcoming others affected your life? Has it changed your view of yourself, of others, of your church, the world, God?

+ Tell about a time you wanted to welcome another but were unable to. What happened?

+ Tell about a time you feared welcoming another person. What happened?

+ What has helped you welcome others? What has hindered you?

In closing, reflect on your discussion of both sets of questions. What insights about the experience of welcome have emerged? What lessons do you carry from these experiences?

2. Bible Study

Explore Bible passages that speak of the experience of vulnerability, anger, and sorrow: Matthew 26:36–46; Mark 11:15–16; Luke 2:1–7; John 1:14. Discuss:

* How is Jesus' humanity depicted?

* What in the passage resonates with your own experience of your humanity/finitude?

* What difference does it make to you that God welcomes these human experiences?

3. Connecting the Dots

Discuss the connections between our experience of God's welcome and the ways we offer welcome. These questions may help:

* How has God's welcome in your life shaped the way you welcome others?

* How does God's welcome within your church family shape the way your church welcomes?

4. Salvation Talk

Discuss the word "salvation." Begin with simple word association. Brainstorm a list of responses to the word "salvation" on newsprint for the group to see. Discuss the list. For further conversation, use these springboard questions:

* How do you understand salvation? What does it mean to you?

* What about the word "salvation" is confusing or uncomfortable?

* Do you agree or disagree with the definition of salvation as "the continual presence and activity of God in our lives" on page 101, and why?

- What do you make of the notion of salvation as God's salve-ing, or healing? How does that ring true to your experience?

- In what ways is salvation a useful word in your faith life?

5. A Welcome Feast

Hold a welcome feast, a time for food and fellowship. The children's mural of "The Land of Welcome" might be presented or consecrated, "telling times" can be offered, or a "wall of welcome" can be posted with blank butcher paper for participants to add their own words, symbols, or drawings of God's welcome.

6. The E-Word

Discuss the word "evangelism." Begin with simple word association. Brainstorm a list of responses to the word "evangelism" on newsprint for the group to see. Discuss the list. For further conversation, use these springboard questions:

- What do you think about the definition of evangelism as "living the good news"?

- Do you have a sense of good news in your life? Describe it.

- What are your anxieties about evangelism?

- What forms has evangelism taken in your experience?

- What are your desires about evangelism?

- What do you need in order to share/live the good news?

7. Taking Stock

Take stock of what your congregation currently teaches through the worship service about salvation. Collect worship bulletins from several weeks and distribute them, along with hymnals and Bibles, to the group. In small groups or plenary, review the bulletins, including biblical and hymn texts. Discuss the following questions:

- What do you currently teach in worship about salvation?

- In these sources, is salvation strictly "going to heaven"? Is it something else, and if so, what?

- What is missing in these worship services that you would want to add about salvation?

8. 50/50?

This exercise explores our notions about the Incarnation, God made flesh in Jesus Christ.

First, give the participants a piece of paper and ask them to draw two circles, one depicting Jesus' humanity (labeled H) and one depicting Jesus' divinity (labeled D), in relation to each other. For example, one might draw two overlapping circles or two separate circles. The size, position, and shape of the circles can be used to represent the relationship between these two aspects of the Incarnation. Second, ask them to assign a percentage to each circle, based on their understanding of the Incarnation. For example, if they think of Jesus as 30 percent human and 70 percent divine (or 50/50 or 80/100), they would assign those percentages to each circle accordingly. Percentages need not be limited by the sum of 100. This is an exploratory exercise for discussion. Third, ask the participants in pairs, to share their diagram and the notions it represents.

In plenary, discuss insights gained from sharing diagrams. Close the discussion with the questions: In what ways is the teaching of the Incarnation important to you?

9. Monday Morning Connections

How do you share God's welcome through your weekly activities at school, work, or home?